OUR
BICENTENNIAL
CRISIS

OUR BICENTENNIAL CRISIS

A Call to Action for
Harvard Law School's
Public Interest Mission

Pete Davis
The Harvard Law Record

The Harvard Law Record Corporation
1563 Massachusetts Avenue
Cambridge, MA 02138

Printed in the United States of America.

ISBN-13: 978-0-692-97027-0

Library of Congress Control Number: 2017916238

The Harvard Law Record is the oldest law school-affiliated newspaper in the United States. It has been published since 1946, and its contributors have included presidential candidate Ralph Nader, Supreme Court justice William Rehnquist, notable law professors, and writers who have gone on to win Pulitzer, O. Henry, and PEN Prizes. The newspaper has been the recipient of several American Bar Association journalism awards over the past decade.

Visit www.HLRecord.org for more information.

Contact the author at PeDavis@JD18.law.harvard.edu or through www.HLSReport.org.

TABLE OF CONTENTS

"If we are to keep our democracy, there must
be one commandment:
Thou shalt not ration justice."

LEARNED HAND, HARVARD LAW CLASS OF 1896

"To educate leaders who contribute
to the advancement of justice
and the well-being of society."

THE HARVARD LAW SCHOOL MISSION STATEMENT

1.

HOLMES' CHALLENGE

Harvard Law School prides itself on being a leader in legal education. As we, the Harvard Law School community, celebrate our bicentennial this year, we will surely be reminded of the lengthy list of Harvard Law's historic accomplishments. We are the longest continuously running law school in the United States. It was our Christopher Columbus Langdell who not only standardized the content of the first-year legal curriculum, but also, in joining the case method to the Socratic method, invented the dominant pedagogical model through which that curriculum was to be, and still is, transmitted to American law students. Our Legal Aid Bureau, Law Review, law school newspaper, alumni association, and public interest placement office are each the longest running of their kind.[1] "By the visibility of our example," Joel Seligman writes in *The High Citadel*, Harvard Law School has "dominated American legal education."[2]

When at our best, we have remained relevant for two centuries by acknowledging and responding to what our own Oliver Wendell Holmes, Jr. once called "the felt necessities of the time."[3] When the economy modernized and nationalized at the

---

1 This essay was written with the help of research and aid from Douglas Grant.

2 Joel Seligman, *The High Citadel: The Influence of Harvard Law School* (1978).

3 Oliver Wendell Holmes, Jr., *The Common Law 1-2* (1881)

turn of the twentieth century, Dean Roscoe Pound worked to have Harvard Law follow suit. When the New Deal called for supplementing the study of the common law with the study of legislation and regulation, we added courses on administrative law and statutory interpretation. In the reformist 1960s, Harvard Law students formed the Black Law Students and Women's Law Associations, pressed for clinics in environmental and consumer protection, and forced the administration to accept a pluralist approach to legal curriculum and campus life. In the late 1990s, while many were dismissing cyberlaw as a niche subfield—in one judge's argument, the concept of "cyberlaw" would be as useful as the concept of "horse law"—we were presciently launching the Berkman Center for Internet & Society to address the unique legal quandaries of the digital age.[4]

If we wish to continue this tradition of leadership in legal education into our third century, we must take up the task of addressing and responding to today's most pressing legal needs. Indeed, if we aim to remain relevant during our tricentennial, the most important question we should be asking ourselves during our bicentennial is the one that would make Holmes proud: *What are the felt necessities of our time?*

---

4 Amy Harmon, The Law Where There Is No Land; a Legal System Built on Precedents Has Few of Them in the Digital World, *The New York Times*, Mar. 16, 1998 (1998), http://www.nytimes.com/1998/03/16/business/law-where-there-no-land-legal-system-built-precedents-has-few-them-digital-world.html?pagewanted=2.

2.

THE CRISIS OF OUR TIME
MASS EXCLUSION FROM LEGAL POWER

Our generation has witnessed a widespread collapse in trust in the national institutions that unite and empower America. Gallup reports that Americans' average confidence in U.S. institutions—measured through an index of 14 key institutions, from banks to newspapers to the medical system—languishes at 32 percent.[5] Most Americans have come to view our national systems as closed cartels that serve the few rather than open forums that empower the many. The more that Americans lose faith in our institutions, the more cordoned off those institutions become—and the more alienated Americans feel from them. This vicious cycle has not only left us to navigate the confounding forces of modern life alone; it has also left us susceptible to demagogues who, instead of doing the hard work of re-opening these institutions to us, further divide and alienate us. With the doors of our nation's institutions closed to her, the average American is left outside asking: *"What is America to me?"*

Our legal system has not been spared in this collapse. Trust in the judicial branch is down 12 percentage points from 1999.[6]

---

5 Jim Norman, Americans' Confidence in Institutions Stays Low, *Gallup*, June 13, 2016 (2016), http://www.gallup.com/poll/192581/americans-confidence-institutions-stays-low.aspx.

6 Jeffrey M. Jones, Trust in U.S. Judicial Branch Sinks to New Low of 53%, *Gallup*, Sept. 18, 2015 (2015), http://www.gallup.com/poll/185528/trust-judicial-branch-sinks-new-low.aspx.

Only 23 percent of Americans say they trust the criminal justice system a "great deal" or "quite a lot."[7] Our courts and legislatures are viewed as tools of the few, monetized at the expense of the many. To the average citizen, justice is inaccessible.

Indeed, the most serious crisis in American law today—the "felt necessity" most relevant to the American public—is that the vast public's legal needs go unmet and legal interests go unadvanced. Millions of Americans are excluded from legal power by their inability to afford a personal lawyer, the lack of career public-minded lawyers representing their interests, and the procedural coup by corporate interests to limit the use of tort and contract law to advance public interests. Georgetown's David C. Vladeck summarized the crisis well:

> For most Americans legal services are generally unavailable, not by reason of their poverty—most of these people are not poor—but simply because they are not wealthy. (I call these people "the un-rich"). Indeed, the difficulty of finding affordable legal services for most Americans is so profound that they cannot afford anything but the most routine legal services (e.g., the preparation of a will), and the poor, unless they are the lucky ones who win the legal services lottery, are simply denied access to the justice system altogether.[8]

2a. Mass exclusion from legal power in the criminal justice system

In the criminal justice system, the lived consequences of this mass exclusion from legal power is ghastly. As Fordham Law

---

7 *Gallup* on Institutional Confidence.

8 David C. Vladeck. Hard Choices: Thoughts for New Lawyers, 10 *Kansas Journal of Law & Public Policy* 351, 351-68 (2000), http://scholarship.law.georgetown.edu/cgi/viewcontent.cgi?article=1270&context=facpub.

professor John Pfaff notes in his 2016 *New York Times* op-ed "A Mockery of Justice for the Poor," since 1995, real spending on indigent defense has fallen even as the number of felony cases has increased by almost 40 percent and the number of prosecutors hired has risen.[9] The public defenders at the frontlines of the system know the indignities of this funding gap all too well. In Fresno, California, 60 public defenders work 42,000 cases per year.[10] In Missouri, according to a 2014 study, public defenders spend an average of 27.3 hours less per case than deemed sufficient to provide effective counsel.[11] One public defender in Ramsey County, Minnesota calculated that his caseload only allows him to spend about "12 minutes per person" in court each day.[12] In January 2016, the New Orleans public defender's office began refusing serious felony cases because, as *The Daily Beast* explains, "chronic underfunding by the Louisiana legislature had left ... staff unable to handle the caseload."[13] Central California Legal Services' executive director reports that when prisoners write asking for help, "we just write back and say we can't help."[14]

---

9 John Pfaff, A Mockery of Justice for the Poor, *The New York Times*, April 19, 2016 (2016), https://www.nytimes.com/2016/04/30/opinion/a-mockery-of-justice-for-the-poor.html.

10 Gabrielle Canon, Can a Public Defender Really Handle 700 Cases a Year?, *Mother Jones*, July 27, 2015 (2015), http://www.motherjones.com/politics/2015/07/aclu-lawsuit-public-defense-fresno-california.

11 Alex Stuckey, In Missouri, Public Defenders Describe Mountains of Work, Low Pay, *St. Louis Post-Dispatch*, Oct. 19, 2015 at (2015), http://www.stltoday.com/news/local/crime-and-courts/in-missouri-public-defenders-describe-mountains-of-work-low-pay/article_c46b8f10-4f97-5a19-932e-c4c229a3b722.html.

12 Jessica Mador, A Public Defender's Day: 12 Minutes Per Client, *Minnesota Public Radio News*, Nov. 29, 2010 (2010), http://www.mprnews.org/story/2010/11/29/public-defenders.

13 Mark Hertsgaard, New Orleans Public Defender Turns Away Felony Cases, *The Daily Beast*, Nov. 25, 2016 (2016), http://www.thedailybeast.com/articles/2016/11/25/new-orleans-public-defender-turns-away-felony-cases.html.

14 Michael Doyle, Conflict Over Legal Services Corp. Continues to Divide Congress, *McClatchy DC*, June 18, 2010 (2010), http://www.mcclatchydc.com/news/nation-world/national/article24585781.html#ifrndnloc.

As a result of these overflowing caseloads, often the best that public defenders can do for poor Americans hoping to vindicate their rights in the criminal justice system is "meet 'em, greet 'em, and plead 'em."[15] Having a day in court to state your case to a jury of your peers is vanishingly rare: about 97 percent of federal cases and 94 percent of state cases are settled through plea bargains.[16] In a 2015 *Harvard Law Review* article, Harvard Law graduate Alec Karakatsanis describes witnessing this reality during his trips to the South:

> I saw hundreds of defendants in minor misdemeanor cases plead guilty without a lawyer just so that they could finally get out of jail after weeks in custody because they were too poor to pay for their release pending trial, and I saw judges routinely inform jailed defendants that they would refuse to give them a court-appointed lawyer if their families were able to pay a bond to have them released from jail. Local public defenders reported to me that there was often little that they could do anyway even if they were appointed given that they had between 1,000 and 2,000 cases per year and barely any investigative resources.[17]

Indeed, Benjamin N. Cardozo Law School Professor Ellen Yaroshefksy's quip about the New Orleans court system applies to many county court systems across America: "You're not

15 Deborah L. Rhode, Access to Justice, 69 *Fordham Law Review* 1785, 1793 (2001), http://ir.lawnet.fordham.edu/cgi/viewcontent.cgi?article=3709&context=flr.

16 Erica Goode, Stronger Hand for Judges in the 'Bazaar' of Plea Deals, *The New York Times*, Mar. 12, 2012, http://www.nytimes.com/2012/03/23/us/stronger-hand-for-judges-after-rulings-on-plea-deals.html.

17 Alec Karakatsanis, Policing, Mass Imprisonment, and the Failure of American Lawyers, 128 *The Harvard Law Review*, Apr. 10, 2015 (2015), http://harvardlawreview.org/2015/04/policing-mass-imprisonment-and-the-failure-of-american-lawyers/.

operating a justice system here. You're operating a processing system."[18]

State legislators have not gotten the message. In the midst of this crisis, only 2.5 percent of the $200 billion spent in 2008 on criminal justice by states and local governments has been allocated to indigent defense.[19] Forty-three states even require indigent defendants to pay at least a portion of their lawyers' fees, no matter how poor they are.[20] This year, for example, the state senate of Kentucky, where public defenders take 54 percent more cases per year than recommended by national standards, rejected a bill to create 44 new positions in the public defender office.[21]

Perhaps states would reconsider if they understood how much the lack of adequate public defense has contributed to the rise of mass incarceration. As the *Harvard Gazette* wrote in 2016, the statistics on mass incarceration in the United States "are sobering for a republic that celebrates justice, fairness, and equality as the granite pillars of democracy"[22]: our 2.2 million imprisoned Americans account for a quarter of the world's prison population;[23] two-thirds of black Americans with low levels of schooling will be imprisoned during their lifetimes;[24] and incarceration is,

---

18 Derwyn Buntin, When the Public Defender Says, 'I Can't Help', *The New York Times*, Feb. 19, 2016, http://www.nytimes.com/2016/02/19/opinion/when-the-public-defender-says-i-cant-help.html.

19 Oliver Laughland, When the Public Defender Says, 'I Can't Help', *The Guardian*, Sept. 7, 2016, https://www.theguardian.com/us-news/2016/sep/07/public-defender-us-criminal-justice-system.

20 Pfaff, *New York Times*.

21 Alexa Van Brunt, Poor People Rely on Public Defenders Who Are Too Overworked to Defend Them, *The Guardian*, June 17, 2015, https://www.theguardian.com/commentisfree/2015/jun/17/poor-rely-public-defenders-too-overworked.

22 Colleen Walsh, The Costs of Inequality: A Goal of Justice, a Reality of Unfairness, *The Harvard Gazette*, Feb. 29, 2016, http://news.harvard.edu/gazette/story/2016/02/the-costs-of-inequality-a-goal-of-justice-a-reality-of-unfairness/.

23 *Id.*

24 *Id.*

Scales of Justice

National spending on public defense, corrections, and police, in millions

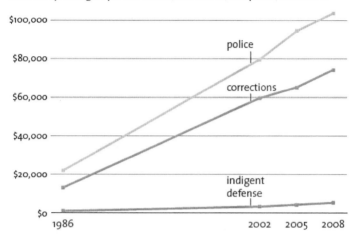

Source: *Mother Jones*, "Charts: Why You're in Deep Trouble If You Can't Afford a Lawyer,"
Jaeah Lee, Hannah Levintova and Brent Brownell, May 6, 2013,
http://www.motherjones.com/politics/2013/05/public-defenders-gideon-supreme-court-charts/

as Harvard professor Bruce Western explains, "socially concentrated among very disadvantaged people."[25] As professor Pfaff's research shows, a primary source of the growth of mass incarceration in the past decades has been prosecutors' overzealous filing of felony charges against arrestees. Consequently, Pfaff notes, "ensuring that prosecutors' opponents are able to do their jobs competently would dampen prosecutorial aggressiveness."[26] Indeed, the mass exclusion of the public from legal power in the criminal justice system has not only perpetuated civil injustice; it has also contributed to what is perhaps our nation's most shameful embarrassment: the ballooning of our prison system.

---

25 Colleen Walsh, The Costs of Inequality: Goal Is Justice, but Reality Is Unfairness, *U.S. News & World Report*, Mar. 1, 2016, http://www.usnews.com/news/the-report/articles/2016-03-01/the-costs-of-inequality-goal-is-justice-but-reality-is-unfairness.

26 Pfaff, *New York Times*.

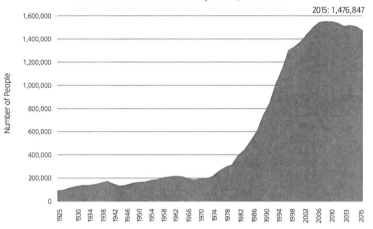

U.S. State and Federal Prison Population, 1925-2015

2015: 1,476,847

Source: The Sentencing Project / Fact Sheet: Trends in Corrections,
http://sentencingproject.org/wp-content/uploads/2016/01/Trends-in-US-Corrections.pdf

2b. Mass exclusion from legal power in the civil justice system

Access to justice under the civil legal system, which lacks the criminal system's precedent set by *Gideon v. Wainwright* that requires states to provide counsel to those who cannot pay, is even worse. Stanford Law School professor Deborah L. Rhode estimates that about four-fifths of the civil legal needs of the poor, and about half of the civil legal needs of the middle class, remain unmet.[27] The Legal Services Corporation's estimate is even more dire: by their count this year, "86 percent of the civil legal problems faced by low-income Americans in a given year receive inadequate or no legal help."[28] Less than $1 out of every $100 spent on lawyers is spent helping advance the personal legal interests of poor

27 Rhode, *Access to Justice*, Fordham Law Review.

28 The Legal Services Corporation, *The Justice Gap: Measuring the Unmet Civil Legal Needs of Low-income Americans*, June 2017, http://www.lsc.gov/sites/default/files/images/TheJusticeGap-FullReport.pdf.

Americans.[29] Since only 1 percent of American lawyers are in legal aid practice,[30] the nation with one of the highest concentration of lawyers provides less than one legal aid lawyer for every 10,000 low-income Americans living in poverty.[31]

When the World Justice Project's Rule of Law Index ranked high-income nations by terms of the accessibility of their civil justice systems, the United States ranked 20th of 23. On their ranking of nations in terms of the ability of people to obtain legal counsel, the United States ranked 50th of 66.[32] As Jim Sandman, president of the Legal Services Corporation, the federal program established to distribute civil legal aid grants, told *National Public Radio* (NPR) for their 2012 report "Legal Help for the Poor In 'State of Crisis'": "We have a great legal system in the United States, but it's built on the premise that you have a lawyer . . . and if you don't have a lawyer, the system often doesn't work for you."[33]

After decades of funding cuts, our civil legal aid system simply does not have the resources to meet the vast majority of our neighbors' legal needs. Take Cleveland, for example: the city's Legal Aid Society, having recently lost more than a dozen lawyers due to budget cuts, had to turn away 57 percent of the 17,000 legal matters brought to them in 2014.[34] "It's rare to have a tenant with a lawyer," Cleveland Housing Court Magistrate Judge Myra Torain Embry told *The American Lawyer*, adding

29 Deborah L. Rhode, *Access to Justice* 186 (Oxford Univ. Press 2004).

30 Rhode, *Access to Justice*, at 4.

31 Justice Index, Number of Attorneys for People in Poverty, National Center for Access to Justice, http://justiceindex.org/2016-findings/attorney-access/.

32 Steven Seidenberg, Unequal Justice: U.S. Trails High-Income Nations in Serving Civil Legal Needs, *A.B.A. Journal*, June 1, 2012, http://www.abajournal.com/magazine/article/unequal_justice_u.s._trails_high-income_nations_in_serving_civil_legal_need.

33 Carrie Johnson, Legal Help for the Poor in 'State of Crisis', *NPR News*, June 15, 2012, http://www.npr.org/2012/06/15/154925376/legal-help-for-the-poor-in-state-of-crisis.

34 Beck, *The American Lawyer*.

that cases where a tenant has counsel usually settle, sparing tenants rapid evictions and harm to their credit.

Or take Philadelphia: the family law unit at Philadelphia Legal Assistance turns away 95 percent of those requesting help. "We don't have the resources," Susan Perlstein explained to *The American Lawyer*. Philadelphia's Women Against Abuse has three lawyers working on protective order cases, but they can "barely put a dent in demand."[35]

Or take Maryland: Joe Rohr, of Maryland's Legal Aid Bureau, told *NPR* that some days they "actually have to close early because of volume."[36] Or take New York: the Task Force to Expand Access to Civil Legal Services estimated that 2.3 million New Yorkers navigate civil legal proceedings without the assistance of counsel.[37] Or take anywhere: as H. Ritchey Hollenbaugh, chair of the American Bar Association's Standing Committee on the Delivery of Services, explained to the *ABA Journal*: "Any local aid office will tell you that at least two-thirds of those who walk through their doors aren't getting help because there aren't enough resources."[38]

This mass exclusion of the public from legal power in the civil justice system has gruesome real-world consequences. As Professor Rhode writes, when the public is denied civil justice lawyers, "domestic violence victims cannot obtain protective orders, elderly medical patients cannot collect health benefits, disabled children are denied educational services, [and] defrauded consumers lack affordable remedies."[39] This exclusion

---

35 *Id.*

36 Johnson, *NPR News.*

37 Rochelle Klempner, The Case for Court-Based Document Assembly Programs: A Review of the New York State Court System's "DIY" Forms, 41 *Fordham Urb. L.J.*, May 27, 2014 at 1189, 1190 (2014), https://www.nycourts.gov/ip/nya2j/pdfs/RochelleKlempner_Court-BasedDIYForms.pdf.

38 Seidenberg, *A.B.A. Journal.*

39 Deborah L. Rhode, *Pro Bono in Principle and in Practice: Public Service and the Professions* (Stanford University Press 2005).

is the denial of hope to someone walking into an overstuffed Baltimore legal aid center hoping to "protect her brother in a nursing home from possible retaliation" because "he was not given medication, he was not fed, he was soaking wet, he had black eyes."[40] It's the failure to vindicate the rights of "a woman being abused who comes in to seek a protective order against an abuser" and is "turned away because there aren't any children involved."[41] It's the closing of the courthouse doors for a Boston tenant who has never been informed that her landlord is legally required to de-lead her apartment if she lives with a child younger than six.

As Harvard Law graduate and consumer advocate Ralph Nader often points out: *without legal remedies, legal rights are meaningless . . . but without legal facilities, legal remedies are meaningless.*[42] If you have a right to redress a grievance against a company that has harmed you, it is meaningless without the ability to sue that company; but even if you have the ability to sue, you are practically unable to do so without a lawyer or a legal group to advance your interests. Put another way by Supreme Court Justice George Sutherland in the 1932 *Powell v. Alabama* decision: the "right to be heard [in legal proceedings] would be, in many cases, of little avail if it did not comprehend the right to be heard by counsel."[43]

Even when Americans are not, say, summoned into court to respond to an eviction notice or seek to get their money back from a company that has wronged them, there is plenty that lawyers could do, and are not now able to do, to affirmatively represent their interests. As Edgar and Jean Cahn explained in

---

40 Johnson, *NPR News.*

41 *Id.*

42 Ralph Nader, *The Ralph Nader Reader* 33 (1st ed. Seven Stories Press 2000).

43 *Powell v. Alabama* 287 U.S. 45 (1932)
http://landmarkcases.org/en/Page/603/The_Evolution_of_a_Decision

their groundbreaking 1964 *Yale Law Journal* article, "The War on Poverty: A Civilian Perspective"—the article that helped inspire the founding of the Legal Services Corporation—there are dozens of ways that community lawyers can advance legal interests in addition to responding to individuals' specific, ad hoc requests. As the Cahns explain, "continuous and effective"—rather than "nominal and sporadic"—lawyering in poor communities can: make government decision-making processes visible to the community; force a community voice into government decision-making processes; compel government responsiveness to community concerns; transfer information from the community to government administrators in legal language; ascertain and vindicate rights in areas of "low visibility" to law enforcement; provide "legal representation in contexts which appear to be non-legal" and where no right can yet be asserted (such as when, say, "a principal orders all boys to come to school dressed in coats and ties without regard for the economic burden this imposes upon the parents"); and help nurture the "growth of embryonic civic organizations." In short, they can "make rights conscious."[44]

Excluding most citizens from civil justice is not only bad for the specific individuals whose rights go unvindicated—it hurts everyone. As Supreme Court Justice William Henry Moody (who himself attended Harvard Law School for four months) wrote in *Chambers v. Baltimore & Ohio Railroad Company* in

---

44 Edgar S. Cahn and Jean C. Cahn, *The War on Poverty: A Civilian Perspective*, 73 The Yale L. J. (1964), https://www.jstor.org/stable/794511. To provide a recent example, a Seton Hall University School of Law study of 40,000 residential eviction proceedings carried out in Essex County in 2014, showed that only .002% of tenants cited the "implied warranty of habitability" defense, "which allows for tenants to legally withhold rent if they are subjected to substandard living conditions." It is highly unlikely that this is because only 80 of 40,000 cases had substandard living conditions—it is much more likely that a lawyer was not present to make this right conscious. [Michael Ricciardelli, Research Shows Tenants Don't Know Their Rights, *Seton Hall University*, Oct. 4, 2016, https://www.shu.edu/news/research-shows-tenants-dont-know-rights.cfm.]

1907: "the right to sue and defend" is "conservative of all other rights, and lies at the foundation of an orderly government."[45] Put another way by Rhode: "Law is a public good: protecting legal rights often has value beyond what those rights are worth to any single client."[46] As our former Dean Martha Minow pointed out in a 2014 *Boston Globe* op-ed calling for increased funding for civil legal aid, this public good has a real dollar value: "every dollar spent on legal assistance for low-income individuals returns between $2 and $5" to the government in "savings to foster care, emergency housing, emergency health care, other social services, and economic growth."[47]

Of course, the converse of these sentiments is also true: when legal rights are not protected, that public value is lost; when the right to sue and defend erodes, orderly government does, too. Take as a prime example one of the largest forms of theft in America today: wage theft. Researchers estimate that $20-50 billion in wages are stolen from American workers by their employers annually. Yet only a small fraction, a little less than $1 billion, of that stolen property is recovered each year in civil suits or by state and federal enforcement.[48] If American workers had anywhere close to the legal power that their employers do, we would not be witnessing such a corporate crime wave. But such is the case for wage workers—as it is for victims of black lung disease,[49] farmers entering into binding indemnity agree-

---

45 *Chambers v. Baltimore & Ohio R. Co.* 207 U.S. 142 (1907)

46 Rhode, *Access to Justice* (book), 11.

47 Martha Minow, We Must Ensure Everyone Has Access to Equal Justice, *Boston Globe*, Oct. 23, 2014, https://www.bostonglobe.com/opinion/2014/10/23/must-ensure-everyone-has-access-equal-justice/pZxzjjHhRoGI8900lZTnhP/story.html.

48 Jeff Spross, One of the Biggest Crime Waves in America Isn't What You Think It Is, *The Week*, Aug. 15, 2016, http://theweek.com/articles/642568/biggest-crime-waves-america-isnt-what-think.

49 Brenda Wilson, Black Lung Compensation an Uphill Battle for Miners, *NPR News*, Apr. 27, 2010, http://www.npr.org/templates/story/story.php?storyId=126303910.

ments,[50] and the multitudes of other unorganized, underfunded *manys* victimized by organized and well-funded *fews*—living during our crisis of mass exclusion from legal power in the civil justice system. Civil aid lawyers are private law enforcement officers. If we do not have enough of them, we make it easier for the powerful to get away with breaking the law.

2c. Mass exclusion from legal power in the political system

In his upcoming paper, "Power: A Prudential Perspective," Harvard professor and democratic theorist Archon Fung proposes an illuminating new model for understanding modern power and politics: *the four levels of power.*[51]

Fung's first level of power is "everyday lives": how power is structured in the day-to-day lives of people aiming to achieve their personal goals. *Can a small business get a loan? Can a victim of domestic violence get protection?* Fighting on the first level of power is what some activists refer to as "retail justice": achieving victories for individuals and small groups.

Fung's second level of power is "covering policies": the "general laws and policies that make it more or less difficult for those people to advance their interests." This is the level where the policy fights occur, in government structures that are both public (legislatures, appellate court cases, executive branch decisions) and private (corporate policies and actions). Fighting on this level of power is what some activists refer to as "wholesale justice": achieving victories *en masse* for whole classes of people.

Fung's third level of power is "structures": "the rules of engagement—the parameters and terrain—that govern the contest between groups and organizations that advocate for individuals at the first level and seek to shape the laws and

---

50 Ralph Nader, Suing for Justice, *Harper's Magazine*, http://harpers.org/archive/2016/04/suing-for-justice/3/.

51 Archon Fung, forthcoming paper: "Power: A Prudential Perspective"

policies constituting the second level of power." It is the level concerned with questions of, say, how elections and parties are structured, to what extent money or fame translates into political power, or how difficult it is to form and fund labor unions or industry associations.

Fung's fourth and final level of power is "beliefs, values, and ideologies": the cultural fights over the ideals and understandings that frame what is legitimate and important to the public. Just as structural power leads to policy outcomes, ideological power leads to structural power. If one has a cause resonant with the dominant ideology, they are better able to mobilize structural elements—like money, volunteers, and votes—toward it.

Fung's model helps explain the importance of what has come to be called "public interest" legal work. Most of what today is called "public interest lawyering" engages in struggles on the first level of power: representing indigent clients in court to vindicate their individual rights. However, when Ralph Nader re-popularized the concept of "public interest law" in the 1960s, he did so specifically to clarify an important distinction between the "retail" legal services work for impoverished Americans and the "wholesale" work of changing policies, structures, and beliefs. To be a public interest lawyer is to engage in zealous advocacy to advance the legal interests of the public at all four levels of power.

Unfortunately, the mass exclusion from legal power in the criminal and civil justice systems—the first level arenas where citizens should be able to vindicate their rights—stems from a mass exclusion from legal power in politics at these higher levels of power.

The legal community sustains this exclusion despite the appeals of various leaders throughout our profession's history to our higher calling as public-minded "officers of the court." "We lawyers are servants of society," Woodrow Wilson wrote in "The Lawyer and the Community" in 1910. To Wilson, lawyers have duties that are "much larger ... than the mere advice of private clients." We must "give expert and disinterested advice to those who purpose progress and the readjustment of the frontiers of justice."

Wilson worried that "lawyers have been sucked into the maelstrom of the new business system," becoming solely "experts in some special technical field." In doing so, they risked losing their role as "general counsellors of right and obligation" who "concern themselves with the universal aspects of society." As lawyers retreated from politics, society had "lost its one-time feeling for law as the basis of its peace, its progress, its prosperity." To regain that feeling, we must:

> recall lawyers to the service of the nation as a whole, from which they have been drifting away; to remind them that, no matter what the exactions of modern legal business, no matter what or how great the necessity for specialization in their practice of the law, they are not the servants of special interests, the mere expert counsellors of this, that or the other group of business men; but guardians of the general peace, the guides of those who seek to realize by some best accommodation the rights of men.

Reminding his fellow lawyers who they truly serve, Wilson concluded: "we are servants of society, the bond-servants of justice."[52]

Five years earlier, Harvard Law graduate Louis Brandeis expressed a similar sentiment. "Instead of holding a position of independence, between the wealthy and the people, prepared to curb the excesses of either," Brandeis told the Harvard Ethical Society in 1905, "able lawyers have, to a large extent, allowed themselves to become adjuncts of great corporations and have neglected the obligation to use their powers for the protection

---

52 Woodrow Wilson, The Lawyer and the Community, 192 The North American Review 604 (1910), http://www.jstor.org/stable/25106795?seq=1#page_scan_tab_contents.

of the people." "We hear much of the 'corporation lawyer,'" he decried, "and far too little of the 'people's lawyer.'" The Bar, Brandeis lamented, had, "with few exceptions, not only failed to take part in constructive legislation designed to solve in the public interest our great social, economic and industrial problems; but they have failed likewise to oppose legislation prompted by selfish interests." In political fights, at higher levels of power than court-room fights, lawyers had, in Brandeis' eyes, shown "disregard of common weal . . . erroneously [assuming] that the rule of ethics to be applied to a lawyer's advocacy is the same where he acts for private interest against the public, as it is in litigation between private individuals." Against this trend, he called on young lawyers to "do a great work for this country" and give "adequate legal expression" to "the aspirations of the people."[53]

Decades later, Ralph Nader revived Justice Brandeis' civic-minded call, recruiting dozens of young lawyers to shake up Washington in the name of "the public interest." His "new generation of lawyers" would be a civic-minded counterforce to a system where "all the lawyers are on the corporation's side"[54]:

> Lawyers labored for polluters, not anti-polluters; for sellers, not consumers; for corporations, not citizens; for labor leaders, not rank and file; for, not against, rate increases or weak standards before government agencies, for highway builders, not displaced residents, for, not against, judicial and administrative delay, for preferential business access to government and against equal citizen access to the same government, for agricultural subsidies to the rich, but not

53 Louis Brandeis, The Opportunity in the Law, Speech to the Harvard Ethical Society, May 4, 1905, https://louisville.edu/law/library/special-collections/the-louis-d.-brandeis-collection/business-a-profession-chapter-20.

54 Jack Doyle, Nader's Raiders, 1968-1974, *PopHistoryDig.com*, Mar. 31, 2013, http://www.pophistorydig.com/topics/naders-raiders-1968-1974/ (referencing October 1969 *Life Magazine* article).

food stamps for the poor, for tax and quota privileges, not for equity and free trade.[55]

Summarizing, Nader wrote that there were "massive public interests deprived of effective legal representation."[56] Why did he think this was so? As Nader explained to *Life Magazine* in 1969, "most lawyers are too hung up on clients." There needed to be, Nader argued, "a new dimension to the legal profession," where lawyers "represent systems of justice" on "the public's side," independent of corporate and government interests.[57] This new dimension "does not simply extend to those groups or individuals who cannot afford a lawyer"—rather, it extends beyond "to the immense proliferation of procedural and substantive interests which go to the essence of the kind of society we will have in the future, but which have no legal representation."[58] To put Nader's idea in Fung's terms, the public needed lawyers fighting for them in the higher level arenas of policy, structure, and ideology.

Today, very few are doing so. Data from a 2005 American Bar Association survey suggests that less than 1 percent of lawyers are professionally representing the public interest in the political system, independent of business or government. Eighty-three percent of lawyers are in private practice or industry, 11 percent are in government or the judiciary, 4 percent are retired, and the final three percent were split between education, legal aid, and the only survey option which might resemble Nader's idea of a public interest lawyer: "private association."[59]

As the research of lobbying scholar Lee Drutman shows, the

---

55 Ralph Nader, *The Ralph Nader Reader*, at 392

56 *Id.*, at 391.

57 Doyle, *PopHistoryDig.com* (referencing October 1969 *Life Magazine* article).

58 Ralph Nader, *The Ralph Nader Reader*, at 395.

59 Lawyer Demographics, Year 2016, *AmericanBar.org* (2016), https://www.americanbar. org/content/dam/aba/administrative/market_research/lawyer-demographics-tables-2016. authcheckdam.pdf.

public interest is also outgunned in Congressional debates. Business interests account for roughly 80 percent of all reported federal government lobbying expenditures. Of the 100 organizations that spend the most on lobbying annually, 95 represent business. The types of organized interests who provide a countervailing force to business in policy fights—labor unions, consumer groups, and taxpayer groups—are outspent $34 to $1 by corporate interest groups. Of the 60 corporate lobbyists interviewed for Drutman's *The Business of America is Lobbying*, not a single lobbyist said a union or a public interest group was the leading opposition on an issue on which they were currently working.[60]

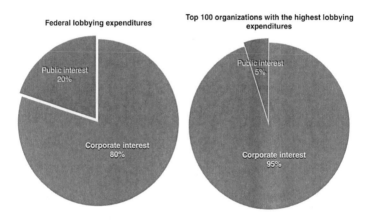

Federal lobbying expenditures

Public interest 20%

Corporate interest 80%

Top 100 organizations with the highest lobbying expenditures

Public interest 5%

Corporate interest 95%

Source: Lee Drutman, What We Get Wrong About Lobbying and Corruption, *The Washington Post*, April 16, 2015

At Fung's fourth level of power—ideology—private interests have also advanced with little challenge in the legal system. As

---

60 Lee Drutman, What We Get Wrong About Lobbying and Corruption, *The Washington Post*, Apr. 16, 2015, https://www.washingtonpost.com/news/monkey-cage/wp/2015/04/16/what-we-get-wrong-about-lobbying-and-corruption/?utm_term=.bf0cccc95031.

Jane Mayer explains in *Dark Money*, the John M. Olin Foundation, a business-friendly foundation established with money from a chemical and munitions manufacturing fortune, spent $68 million between the years of 1985 and 1989 to underwrite "83 percent of the costs for all Law and Economics programs in American law schools." "I saw it as a way into the law schools—I probably shouldn't confess that," conservative scholar and Olin trustee James Piereson told *The New York Times*. "Economic analysis tends to have conservatizing effects." He later explained his Trojan horse further: "If you said to a dean that you wanted to fund conservative constitutional law, he would reject the idea out of hand ... but if you said you wanted to support Law and Economics, he would be much more open to the idea." "Law and Economics," he continued, "is neutral, but it has a philosophical thrust in the direction of free markets and limited government."

In their book *Agenda Setting: A Wise Giver's Guide to Influencing Public Policy*—a self-described how-to guide for "donating money to modify public thinking and government policy"—the right-wing Philanthropy Roundtable cites Olin's donations to Harvard Law School as one of the Foundation's "savviest interventions":

> The foundation offered to fund a new program in law and economics with a multiyear grant ... Harvard president Derek Bok leaped at the offer. The [HLS-based] John M. Olin Center for Law, Economics, and Business eventually received more than $18 million from the Olin Foundation, and it was a smashing success. By 2005, the number of Harvard faculty whose central interests could be defined within the sphere of law and economics had jumped to 23. More than four dozen alumni of the program had been hired as faculty at other law schools, bringing law and economics insights to top schools like University of California-Berkeley

and Michigan. The John M. Olin Fellowships for students have turned into springboards to prominent clerkships.[61]

To supplement their evangelization to law students, the Olin foundation began funding Law and Economics seminars for judges: "two-week-long, all-expenses-paid immersion training in Law and Economics usually in luxurious settings like the Ocean Reef Club in Key Largo, Florida." Major corporations joined in the funding: the underwriters of such recent seminars—which involved, Mayer explains, golf, swimming, fancy dinners and discussions on the downsides of "environmental and labor laws"— included ExxonMobil, Shell Oil, Pfizer, and State Farm.[62]

A few decades after their initial donations, the legal ideology best aligned with corporate interests had, in the words of Steven Teles, "rapidly moved from insurgency to hegemony."[63] There is no comparable example of this level of funding used to intervene in legal thought on the side of less funded and less organized, yet more populated groups, such as workers, consumers, tenants, prisoners, and everyday victims of torts.

This ideological and political assault has been crippling longstanding tools of public power. Take tort law, for example. It evolved over centuries into a revolutionary civic tool to empower ordinary citizens to collect information, redress grievances and make rights real. Through the mid-twentieth century, it expanded in the public interest: comparative negligence empowered plaintiffs to recover some damages despite their own contributory negligence; strict liability standards held manufacturers liable for dangerous defects; and civil procedure was amended in the 1960s to make filing class actions easier.

---

61 John J. Miller and Karl Zinsmeister, Agenda Setting: A Wise Giver's Guide to Influencing Public Policy, Chapter 3 (The Philanthropy Roundtable 2015).

62 Jane Mayer, *Dark Money.*

63 *Id.*

However, in recent decades, this tide has turned. First, corporate law firms have innovated and widely distributed compulsory fine-print arbitration clauses that re-route most aggrieved customers from the courthouse to arbitration tribunals biased toward corporate interests. Second, a corporate-sponsored "tort reform" movement has pushed thirty-eight states to pass laws limiting citizens' abilities to seek adequate damages from corporations that have wronged them. Third, the Supreme Court has, in recent years, tightened rules on class-action lawsuits to the advantage of corporate defendants.[64]

Take antitrust as another example. Whereas antitrust law originally emphasized firm size or market share—the political and economic power of firms—it shifted in the latter decades of the twentieth century to focus on price and efficiency. As a result, corporations could merge and grow as big as they wanted, as long as they could show that their increased size was the result of "natural efficiencies" that delivered low prices. As Open Markets Institute fellow Matt Stoller shows, this corporate-friendly interpretation of antitrust is preserved today by a revolving door between antitrust regulators and corporate law firms—a system he calls the "Democratic Party's deep state." He describes how *four* of the Obama administration's assistant attorneys general for the Antitrust Division of the Justice Department left to join corporate law firms that represent clients regulated by their former department.[65]

When the ABA released a bipartisan Presidential Transition Report on the state of antitrust enforcement to the Trump administration in January 2017, they admitted that voices from both parties had criticized an "absence of vigor and

---

64 See: Ralph Nader, Suing for Justice, *Harper's Magazine*, https://harpers.org/archive/2016/04/suing-for-justice/

65 Matt Stoller, tweet thread, July 30, 2017, https://twitter.com/matthewstoller/status/891660131188060161.

overall ineffectiveness in current patterns of antitrust enforcement" and called for a "radical reorientation of enforcement policy." However, the bipartisan group nonetheless insisted that the "nation's system of competition enforcement has been in good hands, that an arc of continuous improvement and advancement can be discerned that stretches back over many years and multiple administrations, and that enforcement policy should remain firmly tethered to its statutory basis." Of the 19 members who wrote the corporate-friendly report, 12 were corporate interest lawyers, 14 had ties to corporate interest law, and nine had passed through the revolving door between regulatory agencies and corporate interest law firms. None were from public interest organizations designed to speak for the citizen.[66]

Indeed, at all levels of legal power, from civil and criminal courtrooms to congressional offices, from legal thought to ABA reports, the vast majority of Americans are, at best, outgunned, and, at worst, excluded completely.

2d. Canon 8 ignored

Canon 8 of the American Bar Association's Model Code of Professional Responsibility echoes the pleas of Wilson, Brandeis and Nader. "Changes in human affairs and imperfections in human institutions," it reads, "make necessary constant efforts to maintain and improve our legal system ... this system should function in a manner that commands public respect." Lawyers, it explains, "are especially qualified to recognize deficiencies in the legal system and to initiate corrective measures therein." Therefore, lawyers, the Canon impels, "should participate in proposing and supporting legislation and programs to

---

66 American Bar Association Section on Antitrust, Presidential Transition Report: The State of Antitrust Enforcement, January 2017, https://www.americanbar.org/content/dam/aba/publications/antitrust_law/state_of_antitrust_enforcement.authcheckdam.pdf

improve the system, without regard to the general interests or desires of clients or former clients."[67]

Put another way, we are to be not meant to just be *attorneys*— zealous advocates for specific clients—but *lawyers*: caretakers of the justice system. This is what it means to be a *professional*, explains Justice Ruth Bader Ginsburg:

> I tell the law students I address now and then, if you're going to be a lawyer and just practice your profession, well, you have a skill . . .[but] if you want to be a true professional, you will do something outside yourself . . . something to repair tears in your community . . . something to make life a little better for people less fortunate than you.[68]

One would be hard-pressed to find a more significant "deficiency in the legal system" threatening the system's ability to "command public respect" than the mass exclusion from legal power that plagues the system today. And yet, over the past decades, our increasingly wealthy and populated profession has ignored Canon 8's call to vigorously "initiate corrective measures" and "propose and support legislation and programs to improve the system."

Since the 1970s, the Bar has failed to mobilize as Congress and state legislatures have severely cut back funding for increased access to justice. Legal aid funding has reached its lowest level in decades, while the number of people in poverty is at its highest. Funding for the Legal Services Corporation is 25 percent lower, adjusted for inflation, than it was in 1976, the

---

67 American Bar Association, *ABA Compendium of Professional Responsibility Rules and Standards* 286-288 (2008 edition American Bar Association 2007).

68 Kathleen J. Sullivan, U.S. Supreme Court Justice Ruth Bader Ginsburg Talks About a Meaningful Life, *Stanford - News*, February 6, 2017, http://news.stanford.edu/2017/02/06/supreme-court-associate-justice-ginsburg-talks-meaningful-life/ (quoting Justice Ginsburg).

first year of full Congressional funding.[69] Between 2007 and 2016, basic field funding per eligible client dropped from $7.54 to $5.85.[70] In 2012, the Legal Service Corporation's executive director estimated that over 1,200 legal service positions—1 in 7—had been cut in the preceding years.[71] Congressman Joe Kennedy put the shame best in a letter last year to *The New York Times*: Americans spend more annually on Halloween costumes for their pets ($350 million) than on basic field grants from the LSC ($335 million).[72] It is no wonder that a 2012 study found that LSC-funded programs are turning away half of the eligible people seeking assistance.[73]

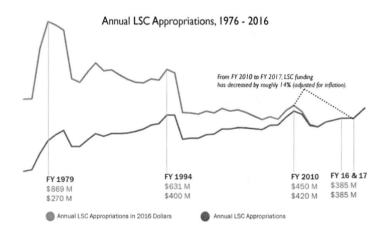

Annual LSC Appropriations, 1976 - 2016

From FY 2010 to FY 2017, LSC funding has decreased by roughly 14% (adjusted for inflation).

FY 1979	FY 1994	FY 2010	FY 16 & 17
$869 M	$631 M	$450 M	$385 M
$270 M	$400 M	$420 M	$385 M

● Annual LSC Appropriations in 2016 Dollars   ● Annual LSC Appropriations

Source: The Alliance for Equal Justice, EJC.org

69 Joe Kennedy III, Access to Justice for All, *The New York Times*, Mar. 2, 2016, https://www.nytimes.com/2016/03/03/opinion/access-to-justice-for-all.html.

70 FY 2017 Budget Request, Legal Services Corporation (2017), http://www.lsc.gov/media-center/publications/fy-2017-budget-request.

71 Carrie Johnson, Legal Help for the Poor in 'State of Crisis', *NPR News*

72 Kennedy III, *The New York Times*.

73 Seidenberg, *ABA Journal*.

Additionally, we have allowed restrictions on who legal aid funding can serve to stymie our profession's ability to serve the broad public. LSC-funded programs may not take cases involving prisoners, most undocumented workers, school desegregation plaintiffs,[74] or those evicted from public housing due to drug use.[75] Even attempts to protect those who go to court without a lawyer have been stymied by our failure to live up to our Canon 8 duties as legal professionals. As Professor Rhode recounts in *Access to Justice*, the ABA has rejected a proposed ethical standard that would have prevented lawyers from "unfairly exploiting" lawyerless litigants' ignorance of the law. Opponents, Rhode writes, argued that "parties 'too cheap to hire a lawyer' should not be 'coddled' by special treatment."[76]

This was not the first time that members of our profession have pushed back against efforts to pass, to quote Canon 8, "legislation and programs to improve the system." As Alan Houseman and Linda Perle explain in their history of Civil Legal Aid, 1960s federal legal services programs "generated substantial opposition within the legal profession" from local bar associations concerned about "competition for clients" and "the impact that representation of the poor might have on their clients, primarily local businesses and governments that might be the subject of lawsuits."[77] This is exactly what Justice Brandeis was referring to decades earlier when he accused lawyers of wrongfully assuming that the ethics of zealous advocacy in court should also apply to politics at large. Corporate-interest

---

74 Rhode, *Access to Justice* (book), at 4.

75 Lisa Weil, Drug-Related Evictions in Public Housing: Congress' Addiction to a Quick Fix, 9 *Yale Law & Policy Review* 161 (1991), http://digitalcommons.law.yale.edu/cgi/viewcontent.cgi?article=1202&context=ylpr.

76 Rhode, *Access to Justice* (book).

77 Alan W. Houseman and Linda E. Perle, *Securing Equal Justice for All: A Brief History of Civil Legal Assistance, Center for Law and Social Policy*, http://www.clasp.org/resources-and-publications/files/0158.pdf.

attorneys, he argued, should not become corporate-interest lobbyists.

Gary Bellow, who co-founded Harvard Law's ground-breaking clinical program, recalled how, in the late 1960s, after the Office of Economic Opportunity moderately increased funding to civil legal aid, the Tennessee bar produced a pamphlet (titled "Et Tu Brute") accusing the OEO of "surreptitiously fostering the socialization of the entire legal profession." The California Bar in the 1960s opposed providing federal funding to support the legal needs of indigent farm workers. "I think the famous quote from the state Bar is," Bellow said in an oral history with the National Equal Justice Library, "'this looks like the financing of one side of an economic struggle by the federal government.'" California Rural Legal Assistance, an organization with which Bellow worked, was even sued by a county bar association on the baseless claims that, as Bellow recalls, "if [they] were allowed to take cases, [they] would act unethically . . . that legal service lawyers would be subject to some outside influences; that they would not be able to be loyal to clients; that they would be over aggressive; [and] that they would be under aggressive." Indeed, when indigent farm workers pushed for a modicum of the legal power that their employers could afford, members of our own profession responded by helping create, in Bellow's words, "a very, very hostile atmosphere."[78]

When Ronald Reagan, who fought against legal aid funding as governor of California, ascended to the Presidency in 1981, he called for an end to federally-financed legal aid.[79] He did not

---

78 Zona Hostetler and Gary Bellow, Interview with Gary Bellow, Nat'l Equal Just. Libr. Oral Hist. Collection, March 17, 1999, https://repository.library.georgetown.edu/bitstream/handle/10822/709332/nejl009_g_bellow.pdf?sequence=3.

79 Stuart Taylor Jr., Legal Aid for the Poor: Reagan's Longest Brawl, *The New York Times*, June 8, 1984, http://www.nytimes.com/1984/06/08/us/legal-aid-for-the-poor-reagan-s-longest-brawl.html.

succeed, but was able to push through a 25 percent budget cut to the Legal Services Corporation (LSC) in his first year in office. Despite President George H.W. Bush's support for the LSC, Reagan's mid-90s heirs continued his crusade to limit impoverished Americans' access to legal power. The 104th Congress, under the leadership of Speaker of the House Newt Gingrich, defunded the LSC's national and state support centers, which had provided important technical assistance and training to federally-funded legal aid lawyers. Worst of all, federally-funded lawyers were prohibited from participating in class action suits, welfare reform advocacy, in-person solicitations, lobbying and rulemaking—limits effectively banning the use of federal funds to achieve "wholesale justice" for poor Americans. As former LSC president John McKay put it, Congress had conveyed the message that "federally-funded legal services should focus on individual case representation by providing access to the justice system on a case-by-case basis."[80]

Those interested in advancing the interests of impoverished Americans at the higher levels of power—by making political, structural, or cultural change—began to view federal funding as a "poison pill," because "any group taking even a single dollar from the LSC could not participate in any of the restricted activities, even if they planned to use state or private funding for those purposes."[81] Indeed, in less than twenty years, President Reagan's dream of crippling federally-funded legal aid for the poor had been realized, thanks in large part to the lethargy of our profession failing to honor its Canon 8 duties to aggressively fight back.

---

80 Houseman and Perle, Center for Law and Social Policy.

81 Kat Aaron, The GOP Plot to Destroy Legal Aid, *Mother Jones*, Feb. 14, 2011, http://www.motherjones.com/politics/2011/02/gop-slashes-legal-aid-funds.

2e. The ability to respond

Responsibility, it has been said, is the ability to respond. As a profession, we have the ability to respond to this mass exclusion from legal power, but we have not taken up our responsibility. The great legal crisis of our time is not a tragic inevitability, but a matter of public choice and priority by our profession. In 2006, non-criminal legal aid government spending per capita was roughly $29.90 in England and Wales, $18 in the Netherlands, $7.20 in Canada and $7 in New Zealand. At the same time, the annual government spending on civil legal aid in the United States was roughly $2.25. This means that Canada is spending over three times as much—and England and Wales are spending a whopping 13 times as much—as the United States is on legal aid for the poor.[82]

Our profession even has the ability to respond without the help of Congress. Last year, the total revenue and revenue per lawyer of *The American Lawyer*'s Top 100 law firms reached a record high $86.7 billion and $907,765, respectively.[83] Between 1986 and 2003, profits for the 100 largest corporate-interest and wealthy-interest law firms skyrocketed from $2.9 billion to $13.5 billion.[84]

---

82 Non-U.S. data from: Roger Bowles and Amanda Perry, International Comparison of Publicly Funded Legal Services and Justice Systems, 2009 Ministry of Justice Research Series (2009), http://webarchive.nationalarchives.gov.uk/20100208125113/http://www. justice.gov.uk/publications/docs/comparison-public-fund-legal-services-justice-systems. pdf, citing European Judicial Systems Edition 2006, European Commission for the Efficiency of Justice (CEPEJ). Non-criminal legal aid spending per capita in report: England and Wales (€23.8); Netherlands (€14.3); New Zealand (€5.6); Canada (€5.7). Author applied 1.256 Euro-Dollar average exchange rate for 2006 to convert to dollars: England and Wales (~$29.9); Netherlands (~$18.0); Canada (~$7.2); New Zealand (~$7.0). U.S. data from: Alan W. Houseman and Linda E. Perle, "Securing Equal Justice for All: A Brief History of Civil Legal Assistance." https://www.clasp.org/resources-and-publications/files/0158.pdf

83 The American Lawyer, The 2017 Am Law 100, April 26, 2017, http://www. americanlawyer.com/id=1202784597030/The-2017-Am-Law-100?mcode=1202615717726.

84 Michael J. Kelly, *Lives of Lawyers Revisited: Transformation and Resilience in the Organizations of Practice* 361 (The University of Michigan Press 2007).

Estimated per capita spending on civil legal aid in 2006

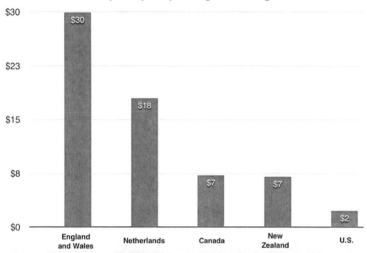

$30	(England and Wales: $30)
$23	
$15	(Netherlands: $18)
$8	(Canada: $7, New Zealand: $7)
$0	(U.S.: $2)

England and Wales — Netherlands — Canada — New Zealand — U.S.

Source: Non-U.S. data: Roger Bowles and Amanda Perry, International Comparison of Publicly Funded Legal Services and Justice Systems, 2009 Ministry of Justice Research Series (2009), http://webarchive.nationalarchives.gov.uk/ 20100208125113/http://www.justice.gov.uk/publications/docs/comparison-public-fund-legal-services-justice-systems.pdf (see note above for currency conversion information). U.S. data: Alan W. Houseman and Linda E. Perle, "Securing Equal Justice for All: A Brief History of Civil Legal Assistance." https://www.clasp.org/resources-and-publications/files/0158.pdf

A decade later, estimates show that those profits have ballooned to about $30 billion annually.[85] With the LSC budget lagging at $385 million, this means that our profession is so profitable that we could, say, more than triple federal legal aid funding with only a 3 percent self-imposed tax on the profits of the 100 most profitable

---

85 Kelly M. Brown, Enter the Disrupters: How New Law Firm Rivals Are Disrupting the Market for High-end Legal Services in the U.S., The Wharton School of the University of Pennsylvania, William & Phyllis Mack Inst. for Innovation Management, MBA Res. Fellowship Papers, May 14, 2014, https://mackinstitute.wharton.upenn.edu/ wp-content/uploads/2014/10/Brown_Enter-the-Disrupters-V2.pdf, citing Am Law 100, ALM Legal Intelligence, 2009-2013 ("Am Law 100 Data"): $75 billion revenue at 40% profits, equaling roughly $30 billion in profits. A similar result is found in data from *American Lawyer*'s AmLaw 100 2013 (http://www.americanlawyer.com/id=1398584264919/) data: total profits per partner multiplied by total equity partners of the Am Law 100 equals roughly $28 billion.

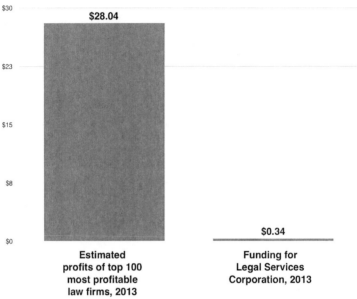

Comparing profits of top 100 most profitable law firms and funding for Legal Services Corporation, in billions

$28.04

$0.34

Estimated profits of top 100 most profitable law firms, 2013

Funding for Legal Services Corporation, 2013

Source: Law firm profits data from:
The 2013 Am Law 100, *The American Lawyer,* http://www.americanlawyer.com/id=1398584264919/;
and Kelly M. Brown, Enter the Disrupters: How New Law Firm Rivals Are Disrupting the Market for High-end Legal Services
in the U.S., The Wharton School of the University of Pennsylvania, https://mackinstitute.wharton.upenn.edu/wp-content/
uploads/2014/10/Brown_Enter-the-Disrupters-V2.pdf. LSC funding data from: Congressional Appropriations, Legal Services
Corporation, https://www.lsc.gov/about-lsc/who-we-are/congressional-oversight/congressional-appropriations.

American law firms. Indeed, the U.S. legal industry, as one of the most profitable industries in the world, has the financial capacity to respond to our access to justice crisis. The choice is ours to take up this responsibility.

When an institution fails to live up to its stated values—when its caretakers abdicate their responsibility—the public loses faith in it. When lived realities contradict the institution's highest ideals, appeals to them ring hollow. As institutional conservatives have taught, every tiny, crooked incident—every little insult to higher ideals that occurs unchecked—chips away at the foundation of the institution, contributing to a potential total collapse. It is apt that the word "corruption" stems from the Latin *corrumpere*: *cor* meaning "altogether" and *rumpere* "to break."

Earlier this year, *Atlantic* writer Conor Friedersdorf shared the story of a twenty-something Donald Trump supporter who believed in Trump not in spite of his anti-democratic tendencies but because of them. He thought of the President's illiberal tendencies as "a feature rather than a bug." *Why?* "When [Trump] undermines rule of law," the young American wrote, "I see ... someone who is undermining a system that has become a game for elites with access to armies of lawyers."[86]

86 Conor Friedersdorf, A Voter in His 20s Gives Up on Liberal Democracy, *The Atlantic*, January 9, 2017, https://www.theatlantic.com/politics/archive/2017/01/a-voter-in-his-twenties-gives-up-on-liberal-democracy/512525/.

3

HARVARD LAW'S
FAILURE TO LEAD

If the rule of law is to be preserved in this country, the legal system must be reformed to extend equal access to justice to every citizen, not just the wealthy few. We do not have much time for this reform: the more that people are excluded from legal power, the less they believe in the legal system and the more susceptible they become to handing over our precious inheritance—the aspiration for equal justice under law—to despots with more immediately satisfying quick fixes than what former President, and Harvard Law alumnus, Barack Obama calls "the hard and frustrating but necessary work of self-government." But the legal profession has been like the proverbial frog in the boiling water: unresponsive, because the threat has grown so gradually.

Our only hope is for a watchdog to wake up our profession. Our nation's law schools—the legal institutions most free from the pursuit of money and state power—must be that watchdog, the conscience of our profession.

Harvard Law School has, at various times throughout its two-hundred-year history, taken this responsibility as the watchdog of the law very seriously. It has baked its desire to lead in this regard right into its mission statement: "To educate leaders who contribute to the advancement of justice and the well-being of society." At its finest moments, it has produced students and staff to whom the broad public could honestly say: "Harvard Law School is extending power to me; Harvard Law School is giving me more faith in the law; Harvard Law School is relevant to me."

And when Harvard Law has taken up this responsibility, it has influenced the whole legal profession, using its large student body, powerful alumni base, representation on federal courts and in government, and cultural heft to make change. When activated, it proves to be an effective fulcrum through which to reform the justice system.

However, when it comes to the legal issue most relevant to the lived experience of most Americans today—the mass exclusion from legal power—we have failed to lead. Instead of leading, we at Harvard Law School have simply mirrored the profession's crisis, producing graduating class after graduating class who, instead of reforming our unequal legal system, quietly files into it. Despite the efforts of a few lone voices for reform and a minority of graduates, most of the educational resources poured into Harvard Law students during their three years in Cambridge still end up being deployed to advance the interests of a wealthy and powerful few rather than to open up legal power to more people in more ways.

Of the 438 employed graduates in the Harvard Law Class of 2015 not pursuing clerkships after graduation, 352 were employed by corporate interest law firms or businesses. That is more than four times as many graduates (86) who joined organizations designed to advance the legal interests of the poor or the public at large (defined as government, non-profit or educational organizations). This means that in any given section of 80 first-year law students, you can expect 16 to work for public interest, governmental, or educational organizations and 64 to work for corporate interest law firms. Indeed, if you walk through the halls of Harvard Law School, less than 20 percent of the students you meet—students being equipped and empowered by a Harvard Law education—will put their degrees to use in organizations dedicated to advancing the legal interests of those outside of a small group of the most wealthy and powerful corporations and individuals.[87]

Harvard Law School, Class of 2015 post-graduation jobs of non-clerking graduates

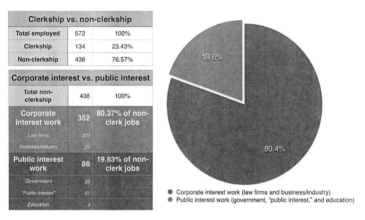

Clerkship vs. non-clerkship		
Total employed	572	100%
Clerkship	134	23.43%
Non-clerkship	438	76.57%

Corporate interest vs. public interest		
Total non-clerkship	438	100%
Corporate interest work	352	80.37% of non-clerk jobs
Law firms	323	
Business/industry	29	
Public interest work	86	19.63% of non-clerk jobs
Government	22	
"Public interest"	61	
Education	3	

19.6%

80.4%

● Corporate interest work (law firms and business/industry)
● Public interest work (government, "public interest," and education)

Source: Harvard Law School - Office of Career Services, Recent Employment Data - Class of 2015 Employment Report at 10 Months After Graduation, 2016 Harvard Law School Office of Career Services Website (2016), http://hls.harvard.edu/dept/ocs/recent-employment-data/.

Whenever this reality of Harvard Law's employment statistics is raised to our school administration, a litany of excuses are presented in response to explain why the issue is more complicated than the stark numbers suggest. The conversa-

---

87 Source for statistics and graphs: Harvard Law School - Office of Career Services, Recent Employment Data - Class of 2015 Employment Report at 10 Months After Graduation, 2016 Harvard Law School Office of Career Services Website (2016), http://hls.harvard.edu/dept/ocs/recent-employment-data/.

tion usually stops there, without much investigation into the alleged "complexities." However, when one examines these responses closely, they do not hold water. Let us put these excuses to rest.

3a. Excuse #1: "Pro bono work and charitable giving blurs the divide"

Corporate interest law firms and Harvard Law administrators like to blur the line between public interest and corporate interest legal work by emphasizing the *pro bono* work and charitable giving of large law firms. However, the evidence shows that the reality does not match the rhetoric.

As Professor Rhode notes in *Access to Justice*, lawyers at the major corporate law firms give less than half an hour a week and half a dollar day to pro bono service and legal aid.[88] At the Top 100 wealthiest law firms, only about eight minutes per day per attorney is given to pro bono work.[89] Only 18 of the nation's 100 most financially successful corporate-interest law firms achieve the ABA Model Rules' goal of fifty hours per year per attorney of pro bono service.[90] During the last decade, as the most profitable firms' average revenues increased by more than 50 percent, pro bono participation declined by a third.[91]

Harvard Law's career services office knows this. In one document on the Washington, D.C. legal market provided to students by the Office of Career Services (OCS), students are reminded that although "firms like to emphasize their commitment to pro bono," they "are increasingly mindful of becoming more like a

---

88 Rhode, *Access to Justice* (book), at 154.

89 Greg Winter, Legal Firms Cutting Back on Free Services for Poor, *The New York Times*, Aug. 17, 2000, http://www.nytimes.com/2000/08/17/business/legal-firms-cutting-back-on-free-services-for-poor.html.

90 Deborah L. Rhode, *Pro Bono in Principle and in Practice: Public Service and the Professions* 20 (Stanford Univ. Press 2005).

91 Rhode, *Access to Justice* (book), at 155

business where billable hours and profitability reign supreme." Students are encouraged not to make pro bono work "the focus of a meeting" with a firm recruiter, because "this could raise concern about your commitment to (or understanding of) practicing in a law firm."[92] This matches ABA survey data, which shows: (1) that only 36 percent of attorneys surveyed do 50 hours or more of pro bono work per year; (2) that younger attorneys are doing less pro bono work than older attorneys; and (3) that the main obstacle to doing pro bono work is lack of time.[93]

When pro bono work is done at corporate interest law firms, it is not necessarily performed in service of the poor. Often, Rhode explains, pro bono reporting is inflated by assistance to family, friends, and charitable causes that largely benefit middle and upper income groups.[94] When the poor are served by corporate firm pro bono, the "boring" retail work of day-to-day service is often ignored: fewer than 10 percent of private interest lawyers accept referrals from official poverty law programs.[95] Rather, "intellectually engaging" work, like death penalty appeals, is what is most often taken up. As a Covington & Burling chairman once told *The American Lawyer*, "the question is, how do we encourage people to see this work for the poor in our local community as sufficiently engaging?" Of course, any help is better than no help, but corporate firm pro bono work, in its current state, is nowhere close to seriously bridging the access to justice gap.[96]

---

92 Dan Binstock, Matt Schwartz, and Justine Donahue of Garrison & Sisson, Washington, DC Legal Market: Spring 2015, 2015 Harvard Law School Office of Career Services Website (2015).

93 The ABA Standing Committee on Pro Bono and Public Service, Supporting Justice III: A Report on the Pro Bono Work of America's Lawyers, American Bar Association website, March 2013, https://www.americanbar.org/content/dam/aba/administrative/probono_public_service/ls_pb_Supporting_Justice_III_final.authcheckdam.pdf.

94 Rhode, *Access to Justice* (book).

95 Rhode, *Pro Bono in Principle and in Practice: Public Service and the Professions*, 19.

96 Beck, *The American Lawyer*.

It would help if the pro bono work of corporate interest lawyers were able to intervene at higher levels of power than individual cases. Occasionally they do, as was the case with, say, Guantanamo Bay detainees in the 2000s and gay marriage litigation in the 2010s.[97] However, as Nader points out, if firm lawyers move beyond "'band-aid law' . . . on a case basis" to "[grappling] with the financial institutions who fund the slum moneylenders for example, or [striving] toward structural reform of a legal institution," then conflicts often arise with their firms.[98] I saw this phenomenon in action at a "learn about pro bono" event put on by a major law firm at Harvard Law's campus last year. When I asked if a member of their firm could, say, use their pro bono hours to give legal advice to Walmart employees aiming to organize a union, the firm responded, "Well, no, Walmart's one of our clients."

Some corporate interest lawyers counter that the best way for them to give back is not through pro bono work, but through charitable giving. If it was actually the case that corporate interest lawyers were using charitable giving to make up for their lack of pro bono work, this might be a good thing. However, as legal services leader Mark Cunha points out, there is too much talk of pro bono work and not enough "emphasis on financial contributions by lawyers or firms and government." Full-time legal services lawyers, Cunha explains, "are more efficient in providing the kinds of services needed by low-income people."[99]

Judge David Tatel of the D.C. Circuit of the U.S. Court of Appeals agrees, arguing in a 2013 speech that "what we need

---

97 See: Neil A. Lewis, Official Attacks Top Law Firms Over Detainees, *The New York Times*, Jan. 13, 2007, http://www.nytimes.com/2007/01/13/washington/13gitmo.html?mcubz=1.; and Joan Biskupic, Top U.S. Law Firms Flock to Support Gay-Marriage Proponents, *The Huffington Post*, August 10, 2014, http://www.huffingtonpost.com/2014/06/10/law-firms-gay-marriage_n_5478107.html.

98 Nader, *The Ralph Nader Reader*, at 394.

99 Beck, *The American Lawyer*.

most of all is dramatically increased lawyer and law firm funding for state and local legal aid programs." As Tatel explained, if the 12 biggest firms in D.C. donated one-quarter of 1 percent of their revenues to legal aid, that would more than double the number of poor Washingtonians served.[100]

But Tatel's admonition was ignored—he heard no response to his speech from the D.C. legal community. "When you look at how little they give," Equal Justice Works director David Stern explains, referring to the corporate interest legal community, "it's pitiful." He continues:

> I have been doing this work for more than 20 years and I am always astounded by law firms talking about charitable giving from a position of scarcity while their partners are bringing home more than $1 million in profits per partner.[101]

Despite many firms recording all-time high revenues and profits, the most generous among them contribute far less than 0.2 percent of their gross revenues to basic legal services for the poor, and many fail to even give that much.[102] Despite revenue of the Top 200 law firms totaling $96.3 *billion* in 2013, only $95.8 *million*—less than one-tenth of one percent—was donated by *all* lawyers and law firms to legal aid funding that year. The bulk of firms' charitable donations are given, according to Susan Beck of *The American Lawyer*, to "other causes, including clients' pet charities and well-endowed law schools."[103]

Worse yet, many legal aid fundraisers are worried that their requests have reached the limit that corporate interest lawyers are willing to part with. The Legal Aid Society of New York,

---

100 *Id.*

101 *Id.*

102 *Id.*

103 *Id.*

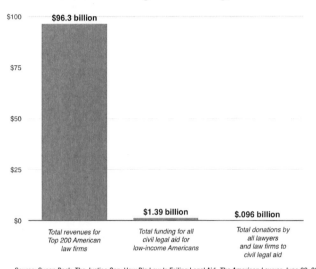

**Comparing: 2013 law firm revenues,
funding for legal aid for the poor,
and donations to legal aid funding, in billions**

$96.3 billion

$1.39 billion

$.096 billion

Total revenues for
Top 200 American
law firms

Total funding for all
civil legal aid for
low-income Americans

Total donations by
all lawyers
and law firms to
civil legal aid

Source: Susan Beck, The Justice Gap: How Big Law Is Failing Legal Aid, *The American Lawyer*, June 29, 2015,
http://www.americanlawyer.com/id=1202730102717/The-Justice-Gap-How-
Big-Law-Is-Failing-Legal-Aid?slreturn=20170107135809

for example, has a giving pledge of $600 per lawyer per year, a level that has not increased since 1996. Though an increase is badly needed to meet the needs of the two million New Yorkers living in poverty, the Society is hesitant to raise its ask because it might compromise their relationship with firms, who might say, they assume, "Enough already."[104] This is all despite the fact that $600 is only four-hundredths of one percent of the $1.3 million average revenue generated by each lawyer at the 18 biggest New York corporate interest law firms.[105] And $600 is also just one-third of one percent of the first-year associate salary at most top law firms, before bonuses.

---

104 *Id.*

105 *Id.*

To give another example, Covington & Burling's chairman reports to *The American Lawyer* magazine that his firm gives 0.11 percent of local revenue to legal aid, but insists that "you can't expect a lot more than what we're already doing . . . you can't expect giving to be unduly high." This message—that slightly more than one-tenth of one percent of local revenues going to support the legal needs of Washington's poorest citizens is unduly high—is coming from a firm that works just a few miles away from Anacostia, where the median household income is $35,082.[106] This message is coming from a firm that has a Political Action Committee that donates tens of thousands of dollars to both political parties to curry favor with whichever wins.[107]

Indeed, contrary to the messages of corporate interest law firms and law school administrators, the line between corporate interest legal work and public interest legal work is not blurred by pro bono work and charitable giving, for there are assuredly not enough hours or dollars coming across the line to come close to making a dent in the access to justice crisis.

3b. Excuse #2: "Everybody deserves a lawyer"

When presented with the disappointing reality of corporate firms' giving, some might respond that simply serving corporate legal interests—even without donating time nor money to legal aid efforts—is serving the public, because "everybody deserves a lawyer." This is true, in the sense that everybody, even the wealthy and powerful, are part of "the public." However, the data on who

---

106 Anacostia Demographics, Point2Homes , https://www.point2homes.com/US/ Neighborhood/DC/Washington-DC/Anacostia-Demographics.html.

107 If one wonders whether the Covington & Burling PAC is the mechanism by which the firm advances their public interest purpose, note that, for example, in the 2012 Virginia Senate race, the PAC donated to both Republican George Allen and Democrat Mark Warner, indicating that the use of the money was not to advance a vision but rather to curry favor with whoever wins. See Covington & Burling 2012 spending at OpenSecrets. org: https://www.opensecrets.org/pacs/pacgot.php?cmte=C00462630&cycle=2012).

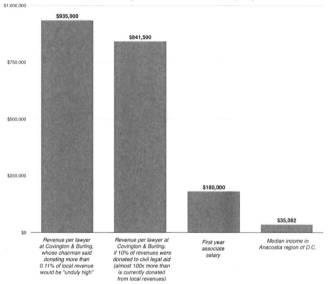

Source: Covington & Burling Law Firm Profile, *The American Lawyer*,
http://www.americanlawyer.com/law-firm-profiles-result?firmname=Covington+%26+Burling.

and where this specific "public"—the clients of large corporate interest law firms—*actually is* show us that the population that Harvard Law graduates serve is tremendously narrow.

Due to the legacy of racial injustice in America, the client base of firms serving the legal interests of multinational corporations and wealthy Americans is disproportionately white. Take the wealthiest Americans who are served by top law firms: despite comprising over 13 percent of the U.S. population, only 1.4 percent of the top 1 percent of households by income are black households. 96.1 percent of the top 1 percent of households by income are white households.[108]

---

108 Antonio Moore, America's Financial Divide: The Racial Breakdown of U.S. Wealth in Black and White, *The Huffington Post*, Apr. 13, 2015, http://www.huffingtonpost.com/antonio-moore/americas-financial-divide_b_7013330.html.

Or take the corporate managers served by top law firms: among Fortune 500 CEOs in 2015, only five were black Americans.[109] As of 2013, 75 corporations in the S&P 500 did not have a single black director.[110]

Or take the stockholders, the legal owners of corporations, who are the indirect clients of corporate interest law firms representing publicly traded corporations. Relative to white Americans, black Americans own less stock in their portfolios. In 2013, only 30 percent of black Americans, compared with 57 percent of white Americans owned stock, either directly or through a mutual fund or retirement account.[111] The wealthiest 10 percent of all Americans, a disproportionately white demographic group, own 81 percent of all shares of stock owned by U.S. households (as of 2010),[112] while over half of American households did not hold any stock at all.[113]

On the other side of the coin, the client base for legal aid and public defense organizations is disproportionately black and Hispanic. In 2011, 45.4 percent of clients served by federally-funded legal aid offices were black or Hispanic Americans.[114] Thirty-six percent of American children living in poverty are

109 Gregory Wallace, Only 5 Black CEOs at 500 Biggest Companies, *CNN MONEY*, Jan. 29, 2015, http://money.cnn.com/2015/01/29/news/economy/mcdonalds-ceo-diversity/.

110 Black Enterprise, Black Enterprise Releases Exclusive Report on African American Corporate Directors, *Black Enterprise*, Sept. 6, 2013, http://www.blackenterprise.com/news/report-black-corporate-directors-study-boardrooms/.

111 Allison Schrager, What the Stock Market Has to Do with Racial Inequality, *Bloomberg*, Jan. 9, 2015, https://www.bloomberg.com/news/articles/2015-01-09/what-the-stock-market-has-to-do-with-racial-inequality-iiborpIV.

112 Robert Frank, The Stock Gap: American Stock Holdings at 18-year Low, *CNBC*, Sept. 8, 2014, http://www.cnbc.com/2014/09/08/the-stock-gap-american-stock-holdings-at-18-year-low.html, citing Edward N. Wolff, economics professor at New York University.

113 EPI, Share of Households Owning Stock, 1989-2010, *Economic Policy Institute*, Aug. 22, 2012, http://www.stateofworkingamerica.org/chart/swa-wealth-table-6-9-share-households-owning/, citing Edward N. Wolff, economics professor at New York University.

114 Public Welfare Foundation/The Kresge Foundation, Natural Allies: Philanthropy and Civil Legal Aid (Public Welfare Foundation/The Kresge Foundation 2013), http://kresge.org/sites/default/files/Philanthropy-and-civil-legal-aid.pdf.

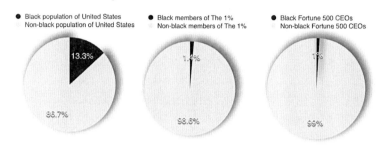

Black representation in
corporate interest law client base

- Black population of United States
  Non-black population of United States
- Black members of The 1%
  Non-black members of The 1%
- Black Fortune 500 CEOs
  Non-black Fortune 500 CEOs

13.3%

86.7%

1.9%

98.6%

1%

99%

Source: Antonio Moore, America's Financial Divide: The Racial Breakdown of U.S. Wealth in Black and White, *The Huffington Post*, Apr. 13, 2015, http://www.huffingtonpost.com/antonio-moore/americas-financial-divide_b_7013330.html; Gregory Wallace, Only 5 Black CEOs at 500 Biggest Companies, *CNN MONEY*, Jan. 29, 2015, http://money.cnn.com/2015/01/29/news/economy/mcdonalds-ceo-diversity/

black.[115] Thirty-eight   percent of state prisoners are black.[116] Despite using drugs at similar rates to American of other races, black Americans comprise 31 percent of those arrested and 40 percent of those incarcerated for drug law violations.[117] In Matthew Desmond's groundbreaking Milwaukee Area Renters Study, the Harvard sociologist found that women from black neighborhoods accounted for 30 percent of all evictions despite representing only 9.6 percent of the population.[118]

---

115 National KIDS COUNT, *Children in Poverty By Race and Ethnicity* (National KIDS COUNT 2015), http://datacenter.kidscount.org/data/tables/44-children-in-poverty-by-race-and-ethnicity#detailed/1/any/false/573,869,36,868,867/10,11,9,12,1,185,13/324,323.

116 Ashley Nellis, *The Color of Justice: Racial and Ethnic Disparity in State Prisons* (The Sentencing Project 2016), http://www.sentencingproject.org/publications/color-of-justice-racial-and-ethnic-disparity-in-state-prisons/.

117 The Drug Policy Alliance, *The Drug War, Mass Incarceration and Race* (The Drug Policy Alliance 2016), https://www.drugpolicy.org/sites/default/files/DPA%20Fact%20Sheet_Drug%20War%20Mass%20Incarceration%20and%20Race_%28Feb.%202016%29_0.pdf.

118 Matthew Desmond, Poor Black Women Are Evicted at Alarming Rates, Setting Off a Chain of Hardship (MacArthur Foundation, How Housing Matters 2014), https://www.macfound.org/media/files/HHM_Research_Brief_-_Poor_Black_Women_Are_Evicted_at_Alarming_Rates.pdf.

Black representation in
public interest law client base

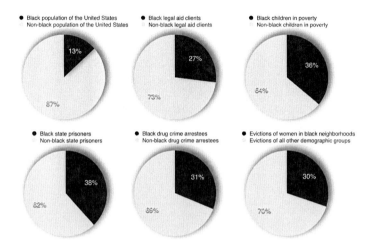

Sources: Public Welfare Foundation/The Kresge Foundation, *Natural Allies: Philanthropy and Civil Legal Aid* (Public Welfare Foundation/The Kresge Foundation 2013), http://kresge.org/sites/default/files/Philanthropy-and-civil-legal-aid.pdf; National KIDS COUNT, *Children in Poverty By Race and Ethnicity* (National KIDS COUNT 2015), http://datacenter.kidscount.org/data/tables/44-children-in-poverty-by-race-and-ethnicity#detailed/1/any/false/573,869,36,868,867/10,11,9,12,1,185,13/324,323; Ashley Nellis, *The Color of Justice: Racial and Ethnic Disparity in State Prisons* (The Sentencing Project 2016), http://www.sentencingproject.org/publications/color-of-justice-racial-and-ethnic-disparity-in-state-prisons/; The Drug Policy Alliance, *The Drug War, Mass Incarceration and Race* (The Drug Policy Alliance 2016), https://www.drugpolicy.org/sites/default/files/DPA%20Fact%20Sheet_Drug%20War%20Mass%20Incarceration%20and%20Race_%28Feb.%202016%29_0.pdf; Matthew Desmond, Poor Black Women Are Evicted at Alarming Rates, Setting Off a Chain of Hardship (MacArthur Foundation, How Housing Matters 2014), https://www.macfound.org/media/files/HHM_Research_Brief_-_Poor_Black_Women_Are_Evicted_at_Alarming_Rates.pdf (eviction data only from Milwaukee).

Given this, one could restate the public interest vs. corporate interest divide in terms of the racial makeup of their respective client bases: four times as many Harvard Law graduates pursue work with organizations designed to serve the legal interests of a disproportionately white client base as pursue work with organizations designed to serve the legal interests of a disproportionately black client base.

Harvard Law graduates are not only serving a narrow public in terms of race. They are also serving a narrow public in terms of geography. Of the 555 new alumni who worked domestically after graduating in 2015, 385 students—69.37 percent of all domestic

Geographical distribution of first post-graduate job of Harvard Law School students

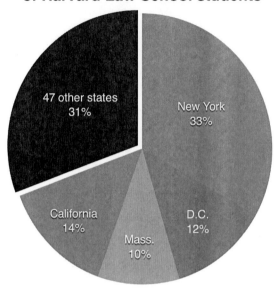

47 other states 31%

New York 33%

California 14%

Mass. 10%

D.C. 12%

Source: Harvard Law School - Office of Career Services, Additional Employment Data, 2016 Harvard Law School Office of Career Services Website (2016), http://hls.harvard.edu/dept/ocs/recent-employment-data/additional-employment-data/.

graduates—worked in just four states: New York, California, D.C., and Massachusetts. This is 3.4 times as many as one would expect if Harvard graduates were distributed proportionally to state population. In fact, fewer graduates in the Class of 2015 went to work in the other 47 states combined (170 graduates) than went to work just in the state of New York (184 graduates).[119]

Harvard Law prides itself on its diversity of inputs: students of all races from all around the country. However, when viewed

---

119 Source for statistics and graphs: Harvard Law School - Office of Career Services, Additional Employment Data, 2016 Harvard Law School Office of Career Services Website (2016), http://hls.harvard.edu/dept/ocs/recent-employment-data/additional-employment-data/.

in light of the narrow range of outputs, a disturbing picture emerges of a school that attracts a diverse set of students from all across the country and sends them to New York to serve a disproportionately rich and white client base. If everybody deserves a lawyer, should not Harvard work to encourage the lawyers it trains to go where people are underserved?

3c. Excuse #3: "Graduates take public interest jobs later"

Sometimes it is conceded that public interest legal work is more aligned with the mission of Harvard Law School than corporate interest legal work. However, this concession is often paired with the argument that students who immediately go into corporate interest legal work after graduation will return to public interest legal work later in life. Again, however, the data show otherwise.

It is a relatively rare event for a Harvard Law graduate who worked in corporate interest law for a few years after graduation to transition into public interest work a decade later. According to Harvard's "After the JD" study, only 7.2 percent of Harvard Law graduates who are working at large firms three years after graduation are working in public interest organizations twelve years after graduation. The same is true for only 4.6 percent of lawyers who are working at mid-sized firms. Even worse, less than 0.2 percent of those surveyed were working in legal services or as a public defender. Indeed, of the *303* members of the 2015 graduating class working in 100+ lawyer firms after graduation, we can expect, if these trends continue, *only 22* to be working in public interest organizations nine years later.[120] Of those 22, maybe one will work in direct services.

The Center on the Legal Profession's 2015 HLS Career Study—which looks at the career trajectories of the Class of

---

120 Private email with member of Center for the Legal Profession, citing internal *After the JD Study* data.

Growth in private interest legal work after graduation among male Harvard Law School graduates

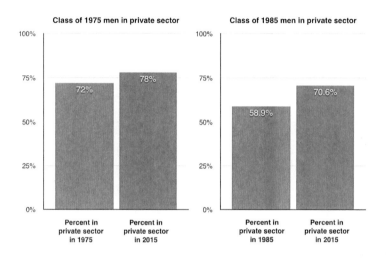

1975, 1985, 1995, and 2000, split by gender—paints a slightly rosier picture, but not by much. seventy-two percent of men in the Class of 1975 worked in a law firm or a business after law school and 78 percent did in 2015. Almost sixty percent of men in the Class of 1985 worked in a law firm or a business after law school and 70.6 percent did in 2015. The same trend continues with the Class of 1995 (from 71.3 percent in 1995 to 86.2 percent in 2015) and 2000 (from 69.9 percent to 70.3 percent in 2015). *More* Harvard Law men, *not less*, are deploying their educations for a business or corporate interest law firm 15, 20, 30, and 40 years after graduation day. By 2015, no class studied had more than 30 percent of male graduates working in public interest organizations.[121]

---

121 David B. Wilkins, Bryon Fong, and Ronit Dinovitzer, *The Women and Men of Harvard Law School: Preliminary Results from the HLS Career Study* (Harvard Law School: Center on the Legal Profession 2015), https://clp.law.harvard.edu/assets/HLS-Career-Study-FINAL.pdf.

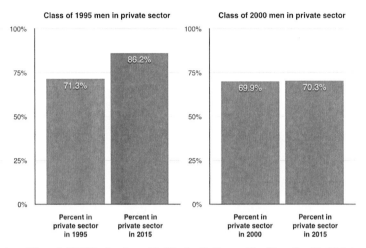

Class of 1995 men in private sector   Class of 2000 men in private sector

Image 13 Source: David B. Wilkins, Bryon Fong, and Ronit Dinovitzer, *The Women and Men of Harvard Law School: Preliminary Results from the HLS Career Study* (Harvard Law School: Center on the Legal Profession 2015), https://clp.law.harvard.edu/assets/HLS-Career-Study-FINAL.pdf

There does appear to be a slight shift away from business and corporate interest law for Harvard Law women. Whereas 65.4 percent of women in the Class of 1975 worked for firms or businesses after graduation, that number was down to 45.1 percent by 2015, with 54.9 percent of the class' women working in public sector organizations. However, that 20 percentage point drop in corporate interest work is not matched in later classes: the Classes of 1985, 1995, and 2000 saw 7, 2, and 13 percentage point drops, respectively, in corporate interest work between their graduation years and 2015. That almost half of women in the Class of 2000 were serving the public interest at work in 2015 inspires hope. However, even just among women graduates, the data dispels the notion that there is a major shift from corporate interest work to public interest work in the years fol-

Growth in private interest legal work after graduation among female Harvard Law School graduates

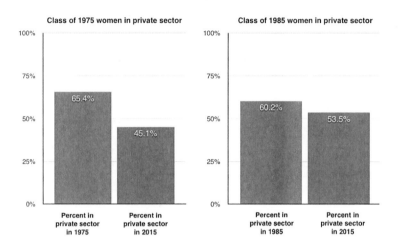

Class of 1975 women in private sector

Class of 1985 women in private sector

lowing graduation. At its measured peak, with the Class of 1975 women, there was only a 20 percentage point shift.[122] (With this data specifically, it should of course be noted that other factors play a role in the gender gap in public interest career trajectories, including gender discrimination and parental leave policies at corporate interest firms.)

The same study compared graduates' plans after graduating law school versus their current plans when they were surveyed recently. The results present the clearest evidence on the lack of any shift back to the public sector. Of graduates surveyed, 214 planned to enter the public sector directly after law school. The number of those same graduates surveyed who planned to work in the public sector today, years after leaving law school? *Also 214.*[123]

---

122 *Id.*

123 *Id.*

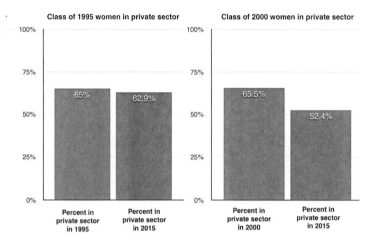

Image 13 Source: David B. Wilkins, Bryon Fong, and Ronit Dinovitzer, *The Women and Men of Harvard Law School: Preliminary Results from the HLS Career Study* (Harvard Law School: Center on the Legal Profession 2015), https://clp.law.harvard.edu/assets/HLS-Career-Study-FINAL.pdf

This data mirrors what Georgetown Professor David C. Vladeck explained in 2000 while reflecting on why corporate interest lawyers do not transition into public interest work. First, he writes, "lawyers trained by corporate law firms will want to practice law in the context of a structured environment" similar to the structure of management and hierarchy in large firms. Second, "the legal knowledge and judgment acquired in big firm corporate/litigation practice does not necessarily translate well to the legal issues confronting individuals." Big firms often represent institutional clients in banking, antitrust, and securities law, for example, which is significantly different from representing individuals in, say, housing court. The third reason, and the least comfortable to discuss, is that "lawyers come to identify with their client-base." As an example, Vladeck remarks: "Put plaintiffs and defense lawyers in the same room," and one will find that "within minutes each group is on its own side." Put in more stark terms: when you hang out with and serve the rich and powerful all day and every day, you lose the desire to transition to hanging out with the less rich and less powerful.[124]

3d. Excuse #4: "Students are free to choose"

Some might say: *fine, corporate interest law and public interest law are different, corporate interest law is monopolizing resources that should be better distributed, and graduates are not drifting back to public interest work after going corporate after graduation. But this is all outside of the institution's purview! Students are free to choose what they want to do with their careers.* This line of argument might be convincing if not for the fact that there is a significant drift from students' professed aspirations at the beginning of law school and their career decisions upon graduating.

Decades of studies affirm this pattern, which has come to be called "public interest drift." In 1978, a study of American law students by Howard Erlanger and Douglas Klegon reported that half of incoming law students wanted to have non-traditional careers with a "social reform component," but only 13 percent actually had jobs in legal aid, public defense, or non-profits after graduation.[125] Between their first and third year of law school, the number of students who reported the opportunity to do pro bono work as "definitely very important" dropped by ten percentage points.[126]

A 1992 study by Robert Granfield found that 70 percent of

---

124 Vladeck, *Hard Choices: Thoughts for New Lawyers*, 2000.

125 Erlanger et al., *Law Student Idealism and Job Choice: Some New Data on an Old Question*, 30 LAW & SOCIETY REVIEW 851, 853 (1996)

126 Howard S. Erlanger and Douglas A. Klegon, *Socialization Effects of Professional School: The Law School Experience and Student Orientation to Public Interest Concerns* (Institute for Research on Poverty: Discussion Papers 1977), https://pdfs.semanticscholar.org/eaa5/oce8e50f72b5bac95ee6afa2d4492d262547.pdf.

entering students expressed a commitment to public interest careers and 55 percent of 1Ls wanted to work in something other than big law firms.[127] However, by graduation, 71.3 percent of men and 65.5 percent of women in the Class of 1995 went on to work in corporate interest firms or business.[128] That means 20-40 percent of students must have shifted during their time at law school.

The Harvard Law Class of 2006's Jenée Desmond-Harris surveyed black Harvard Law Students in the mid-2000s to study public interest drift. Eighty percent of the newly admitted students she surveyed stated that "the opportunity to be of service to society" was among the reasons they came to law school. However, only 58 percent of current students said the same, and only 38 percent of current students reported prioritizing this in their upcoming law-related job. When she confronted students about this shift, she found that they kept their beliefs but changed their method: "I have learned that it is possible to pursue a social justice agenda in any setting … the important thing is to do your job well in any setting that you are in," wrote one student. Another: "I have discovered that corporate influence drives the public agenda as much as political or community actors, so I try to leverage my corporate position to effect change."[129]

If these outside studies are not enough evidence that a significant public interest drift occurs during law school, the Center on the Legal Profession's own study should convince us. Whereas 35.4 percent of newly admitted students planned to work for law firms or businesses after law school, 63 percent planned to work for law firms or businesses by graduation. At

---

127 Robert Granfield, *Making Elite Lawyers: Visions of Law at Harvard and Beyond* (Routledge 1992).

128 David B. Wilkins, Bryon Fong, & Ronit Dinovitzer, *The Women and Men of Harvard Law School: Preliminary Results from the HLS Career Study.*

129 Jenee Desmond-Harris, "Public Interest Drift" Revisited: Tracing the Sources of Social Change Commitment Among Black Harvard Law Students, 4 *Hastings Race & Poverty Law Journal* 335 (2007).

Plan to work in law firm or business after graduation

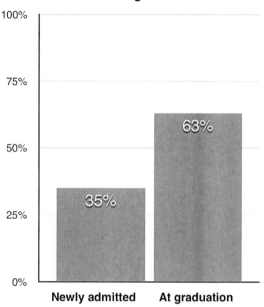

Source: David B. Wilkins, Bryon Fong, and Ronit Dinovitzer, The Women and Men of Harvard Law School: Preliminary Results from the HLS Career Study (Harvard Law School: Center on the Legal Profession 2015), https://clp.law.harvard.edu/assets/HLS-Career-Study-FINAL.pdf

the same time, the number of students that planned to work for the public sector dropped from 33.6 percent to 25.5 percent between admission and commencement.[130]

Something is happening that is shifting students' views between coming to law school and graduating. When confronting this data, it is hard to argue that the culture of our school is not setting corporate interest law as the default option for career choice. One cannot be neutral to this phenomenon. To wash our hands of it is to endorse its thrust.

---

130 David B. Wilkins, Bryon Fong, and Ronit Dinovitzer, *The Women and Men of Harvard Law School: Preliminary Results from the HLS Career Study.*

3e. Excuse #5: "This involves factors beyond Harvard Law's control"

Some admit that we have problem, but argue that the solutions are outside of Harvard Law's control. Again, the reality complicates this excuse.

For example, some say that there are not enough jobs for Harvard Law graduates interested in public interest legal work. When I asked a Harvard Law career services administrator about this excuse, the administrator responded that, yes, if every student is interested in working at "prestigious" public interest jobs in coastal cities, like the New York ACLU or Department of Justice Civil Rights Division, for example, then true, there are not enough job openings. But if half of every graduating class were interested in going to work in public interest and government work in cities and states across the country, then yes, there are plenty of jobs for Harvard Law graduates. Every year, fellowship opportunities, the administrator informed me, are left on the table by each graduating class.

Further belying this standard excuse, other law schools have been much more successful than Harvard at inspiring students to address the access to justice crisis through their career choice. Whereas only 20 percent of employed non-clerking Class of 2015 Harvard Law graduates took up public interest employment (defined as work in, as reported on ABA surveys, governmental, "public interest," or educational organizations), 37 percent of Northeastern students[131] and 35 percent of Georgetown students[132] did.[133]

---

131 Northeastern University School of Law *Employment Summary for 2015 Graduates*, 2016 A.B.A. Section of Legal Education & Admission to the Bar (2016), http://www.northeastern.edu/law/pdfs/careers/statistics-2015.pdf.

132 Georgetown University Law Center, *Employment Summary for 2015 Graduates*, 2016 A.B.A. Section of Legal Education & Admission to the Bar (2016), https://www.law.georgetown.edu/careers/upload/Employment-Summary-for-2015-Graduates.pdf.

133 Graphs and statistics in this section, if not otherwise stated, exclude clerkships from data and measure "public interest" by adding together "public interest," "government," and "academia" in ABA employment statistics.

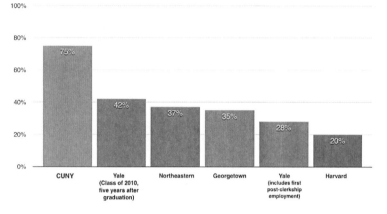

Percent of employed non-clerking graduates in Class of 2015 working in public interest, government or academia

Image 16 Source: City University of New York Law School, Employment Summary for 2015 Graduates, 2016 ABA Section of Legal Education & Admission to the Bar (2016), http://www.law.cuny.edu/career/employment-statistics/employmentsurmma-ry2015classfinal.pdf; https://www.law.yale.edu/student-life/career-development/employment-data/5th-year-career-develop-ment-survey; Northeastern University School of Law Employment Summary for 2015 Graduates, 2016 ABA Section of Legal Education & Admission to the Bar (2016), http://www.northeastern.edu/law/pdfs/careers/statistics-2015.pdf; Georgetown University Law Center, Employment Summary for 2015 Graduates, 2016 ABA Section of Legal Education & Admission to the Bar (2016), https://www.law.georgetown.edu/careers/upload/Employment-Summary-for-2015-Graduates.pdf; Yale Law School, Overview of First Non-Clerkship Job Choices, Yale Law School Website, https://www.law.yale.edu/student-life/career-development/employ-ment-data/first-non-clerkship-employment; Harvard Law School - Office of Career Services, Recent Employment Data - Class of 2015 Employment Report at 10 Months After Graduation, 2016 Harvard Law School Office of Career Services Website (2016), http://hls.harvard.edu/dept/ocs/recent-employment-data/

CUNY Law School students blew Harvard Law graduates out of the water, sending 75 percent of employed non-clerking Class of 2015 graduates to work in public interest, academic or governmental organizations.[134]

Yale, unlike Harvard, measures its students' first non-clerk-ship employment: 28 percent of Yale's Class of 2015 went into public interest, government, or academic work either imme-diately after graduating or immediately after clerking.[135] Five

---

134 City University of New York Law School, *Employment Summary for 2015 Graduates*, 2016 A.B.A. Section of Legal Education & Admission to the Bar (2016), http://www.law.cuny.edu/career/employment-statistics/employmentsurmmary2015classfinal.pdf.

135 Yale Law School, *Overview of First Non-Clerkship Job Choices*, Yale Law School Website, https://www.law.yale.edu/student-life/career-development/employment-data/first-non-clerkship-employment

years after graduating, 42 percent of the Yale Law Class of 2010 were working in the public interest.[136] Even their summer employment numbers beat us: 33 percent of 2Ls in the Class of 2018 at Yale Law, compared to roughly 14 percent of 2Ls in the Class of 2018 at Harvard Law spend their summers doing public interest, government or academic work.[137]

Perhaps the questions we should be asking are: *How have we let Harvard Law School fall so far behind? With Georgetown, Northeastern, CUNY, and Yale beating us in terms of relevance to the legal needs of the many, at what point does Harvard Law risk losing its status as a top-tier law school?*

3f. Excuse #6: "Harvard Law is a path to the upper class"

When all the excuses are finally addressed—when it is admitted that such high numbers of graduates going into corporate interest law is not preferable; when it is admitted that those numbers do not change when measured after graduation; when it is admitted that Harvard might be partially responsible and is falling behind other schools—a final excuse is often proffered: *at least Harvard Law is a path for some students to achieve the American dream.* One is not supposed to raise criticism of Harvard Law's employment numbers, the argument goes, because some students might need these high-income jobs to uplift themselves and their families. Again, however, the data we have belies the notion that most students going into corporate interest legal work after Harvard Law School are from poor backgrounds.

---

136 Yale Law School, *Employment Five Years After Yale Law School,* Yale Law School Website, https://www.law.yale.edu/student-life/career-development/employment-data/5th-year-career-development-survey

137 Yale Law School, *2L Summer Employment,* Yale Law School Website, https://law.yale.edu/student-life/career-development/employment-data/historical-2l-summer-employment-sectors

The office of Student Financial Services (SFS) releases limited data on the economic diversity of each admitted class. However, the data that is available suggests that Harvard Law students are from much more wealthy backgrounds than the average American is. Here is how the logic works out:

According to SFS' website, we know that 45 percent of HLS students qualify for Law School grant assistance.[138] Not much more other data is known on the economic diversity of Harvard Law School, but if we assume that those who qualify for grant assistance arrive from families, by at least Harvard Law's determination, at the bottom 45 percent of some mix of the wealth and income bracket of the school, then we can roughly estimate some of the economic diversity of the school.[139]

The median total income and median net worth of aid recipients' families at Harvard Law School is $95,000 and $175,000 respectively. This means, holding the above assumption, that the median income and median net worth of the bottom 45 percent of Harvard Law School families is $95,000 and $175,000 respectively. This in turn means that 22.5 percent of Harvard students are from families whose income is less than $95,000 and net worth is less than $175,000, which finally leads us to a startling figure: a whopping *77.5 percent of Harvard Law Students are from families that make more than $95,000 a year and have more than $175,000 in net wealth.*

Since the median family income of America is about $54,000,[140] this means that if your family had the median American income and you went to Harvard Law School, you are at the very least in the bottom quarter of the economic bracket of

138 Harvard Law School, *Award Packages*, Harvard Law School Student Financial Services, https://hls.harvard.edu/dept/sfs/financial-aid-policy-overview/award-packages/.

139 Harvard Law School, *Should I Apply for Grant Aid?*, Harvard Law School Student Financial Services, https://hls.harvard.edu/dept/sfs/financial-aid/apply-for-aid/should-i-apply-for-grant-aid/.

140 U.S. Census, *2011-2015 American Community Survey 5-year Estimates*, Census.gov

your class.[141] Even if you were in the fourth quintile of American income (80 percent of Americans having lower income levels than you), you would still be in the bottom quarter of the economic bracket at Harvard Law School.[142]

Since the median net worth of America is $81,456, this means that if your family had the median net worth in America, you would still be in the bottom quarter of the economic bracket of Harvard Law School.[143] In fact, if your family had *double* the median net worth of American families, *you would still be in the bottom quarter of the economic bracket of Harvard Law School.*

If this interpretation of the available information is correct, it would match trends at other Harvard schools. In "Mobility Report Cards: The Role of Colleges in Intergenerational Mobility," Stanford's Raj Chetty, Berkeley's Emmanuel Saez and others found in February 2017 that among Harvard College students born between 1980 and 1982, 70.3 percent of students' parents were from the top 20 percent of the income bracket. In fact, more students' parents were from the top 1 percent of the income bracket (15.4 percent of students' parents) than were in the bottom 40 percent combined.[144]

This interpretation of the available information also matches findings about prominent law schools' generally. UCLA Law

---

141 Pie charts' reference to $90,000 household income being at the 75th percentile in the United States sourced to: Jeremy White, Robert Gebeloff, and Ford Fessenden, What Percent Are You?, *The New York Times*, http://www.nytimes.com/interactive/2012/01/15/business/one-percent-map.html.

142 *Household Income Quintile*, Tax Policy Center, Statistics, http://www.taxpolicycenter.org/statistics/household-income-quintiles.

143 PK, *Net Worth in the United States: Zooming in on the Top Centiles*, Don't Quit Your Day Job, https://dqydj.com/net-worth-in-the-united-states-zooming-in-on-the-top-centiles/ citing: 2013 Survey of Consumer Finances by Board of Governors of the Federal Reserve System, https://www.federalreserve.gov/econresdata/scf/scfindex.htm.

144 Raj Chetty, John N. Friedman, Emmanuel Saez, Nicholas Turner, Danny Yagan, *Mobility Report Cards: The Role of Colleges in Intergeneraitonal Mobility* (2007), http://www.equality-of-opportunity.org/assets/documents/coll_mrc_slides.pdf.

Harvard Law School family income split   **American family income split**

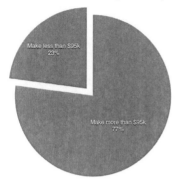

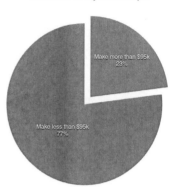

Source: Harvard Law School, Award Packages, Harvard Law School Student Financial Services, https://hls.harvard.edu/dept/sfs/financial-aid-policy-overview/award-packages/; Harvard Law School, Should I Apply for Grant Aid?, Harvard Law School Student Financial Services, https://hls.harvard.edu/dept/sfs/financial-aid/apply-for-aid/should-i-apply-for-grant-aid/; Reference to $95,000 household income being at the 77th percentile in the United States sourced to: Jeremy White, Robert Gebeloff, and Ford Fessenden, What Percent Are You?, The New York Times, http://www.nytimes.com/interactive/2012/01/15/business/one-percent-map.html

professor Richard Sander found than 75 percent of students in the top 20 American law schools are from the top 25 percent of the economic bracket. Even more, over 50 percent of these students come from the top 10 percent of the income bracket. Only 2 percent come from the bottom quarter of the income bracket.[145]

There are indeed examples here and there of Harvard Law students using their education to raise their families up from poverty. However, for the vast majority of students, Harvard Law School is simply preserving class hierarchy: helping already-upper class students maintain—and for some, exceed—the comfortable lifestyles they grew up in.

---

145 Debra Cassens Wiss, Study Finds 'Lopsided' Concentration of Socioeconomic Elites at Law Schools, *ABA Journal*, http://www.abajournal.com/news/article/study_finds_lopsided_concentration_of_socioeconomic_elites_at_law_schools/

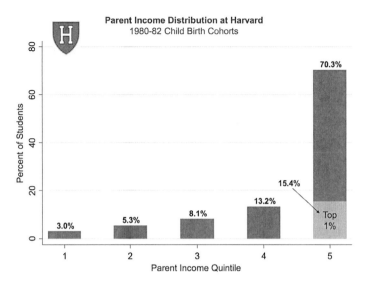

Parent Income Distribution at Harvard
1980-82 Child Birth Cohorts

Source: Raj Chetty, John N. Friedman, Emmanuel Saez, Nicholas Turner, Danny Yagan, Mobility Report Cards: The Role of Colleges in Intergeneraitonal Mobility (2007), http://www.equality-of-opportunity.org/assets/documents/coll_mrc_slides.pdf

3g. Harvard Law through the eyes of the poor

There is an epistemological idea in Catholic social teaching called "the preferential option for the poor." To live by the preferential option is to *see the world through the eyes of the poor*—to build our understanding of how the world works *from the perspective* of the poor.[146] It is the idea that inspired Fyodor Dostoyevsky's remark that *"the degree of civilization in a society can be judged by entering its prisons."*

There is a similar idea in American culture—call it "The Democratic Perspective"—which insists that we are not supposed to see America through the eyes of the extraordinary and powerful,

---

146 See more at Kenneth R. Himes, OFM, *Modern Catholic Social Teaching: Commentaries and Interpretations* 323 (Georgetown University Press 2005), https://books.google.com/books?id=CWt9-LeMuMcC&pg=PA323&lpg=PA323&dq=preferential+option+for+the+poor+epistemological&source=bl&ots=xIeuo7goqm&sig=wZphksFWgqVR2FMAzGzTreuBF8U&hl=en&sa=X&ved=oahUKEwjl7_Sop67SAhVJVWMKHScuD4YQ6AEIHzAA#v=onepage&q=preferential%20option%20for%20the%20poor%20epistemological&f=false.

but rather through eyes of the ordinary citizen and common man. It is the perspective embodied in Eugene V. Debs' insistence that *"I would be ashamed to admit that I had risen from the ranks ... when I rise it will be with the ranks, and not from the ranks."* It is heard when Fannie Lou Hamer said *"Nobody's free until everybody's free."* It is the point of view that made Frederick Douglass ask so powerfully: *"What to a slave is the Fourth of July?"*

What would happen if we saw Harvard Law School through the eyes of the average American in need of legal help? Imagine being a person turned away from an overcrowded legal aid office and learning that 80 percent of students receiving the best legal education in America spend their time after graduating advancing the interests of the wealthy and powerful. Imagine being a person forced to plead guilty to a crime you did not commit after a 15-minute meeting with your public defender and learning that hardly any Harvard Law students go on to work in public defense after school. Does it matter to a refugee that we produced presidents and Supreme Court justices if more of us will spend our time filling out paperwork to help the powerful move money across borders than will spend our time filling out paperwork to help the most vulnerable people at our borders? Does it matter to a Midwestern governor who needs young minds for a fledgling state agency that our job placement in the New York corporate law market is second-to-none? Does it matter to a mother being evicted from her home that Harvard ranks high on the *U.S. News & World Report* list if Harvard is losing out to lower-ranked schools in terms of producing students who help out people like her?

In this bicentennial year, seen through the eyes of America, we risk irrelevance.

Fortunately, this year of reflection is an opportunity to change this situation and reclaim our role as a relevant leader in legal education. To do so, I propose that we reorient ourselves around a simple goal that embodies a commitment by our community to better balance our service to the average American's legal needs. We could call it **The Bicentennial Challenge: let us, as a community, aim to have a majority—51 percent—of Harvard Law graduates devote a significant portion of their careers toward advancing the legal interests of the poor and the public at large.** Since our paths after law school inform the culture of the law school, this simple challenge could serve as a keystone to a larger reorientation of Harvard Law, changing what and how we teach, as well as what we value and fund, so as to better serve our mission of "educating leaders who contribute to the advancement of justice and the well-being of society." If we wish to remain relevant in our third century, such a reorientation is imperative.

4

HOW DID IT GET THIS WAY?

Critiques of Harvard Law's corporate servility are not new. The Class of 1973's Donald Solomon remarked three decades ago that "it is somewhat saddening to think that two-thirds of the seats in every law school are warmed by people whose ultimate goal is not to serve any public interest but to resist collective bargaining, regulate the regulatory agencies, pollute with impunity and fight liability for defective products and industrial accidents."[147] Ralph Nader raised a similar point in the late 1960s, writing that "the greatest failure of the law schools—a failure of the faculty—was not to articulate a theory and practice of a just deployment of legal manpower."[148] He is even spotted making this critique in Scott Turow's famous *One L* memoir:

> "Ask yourself," Nader said near the end, "Shouldn't the best, the brightest, the people who think of themselves as more self-confident, better qualified be the ones to take on those impossible problems? You don't have to lend your power to those huge drug companies that don't care about the public they deal with or to the big law firms that defend them. They can get other people to do that. If you say, 'I will be a

---

147 Seligman, *The High Citadel.*

148 Richard D. Kahlenberg, *Broken Contract: A Memoir of Harvard Law School* (University of Massachusetts Press 1999).

narrow professional, finding pleasure where I can,' then you are demeaning yourself."

Earlier in the memoir, Turow remarks that 25 percent of students did not want to do corporate work, but "expected they would ultimately do it anyway."[149]

If we wish to re-orient the law school, we have to understand what caused this gap between these accounts of our unbalanced service to the legal interests of the wealthy and our school's mission of advancing justice and societal well-being.

How did we get to this point? Of course, there is a simple answer: *people want high salaries.* But to stop our search there is to abdicate our responsibility as a mission-driven institution in a justice-seeking profession. Alfred North Whitehead once said that "duty arises from our potential control over the course of events."[150] Here, I aim to illuminate four areas in which our community has potential control over the course of events and therefore has a duty: (1) a *culture* that fails to spark public spiritedness; (2) a *curriculum* that pacifies students; (3) a *career system* that nudges toward corporate law, and (4) a *cost structure* that dissuades students from public interest work.

4a. A culture that fails to spark public-spiritedness

The drift from public interest values to corporate interest employment during students' three years at Harvard Law School is aided by a culture that undervalues public spiritedness. The source of this stultifying culture has been a concern to Harvard leaders for decades. On the 150th anniversary of Harvard Law School, Dean Erwin Griswold reflected:

---

149 Scott Turow, *One L: The Turbulent True Story of a First Year at Harvard Law School* (G. P. Putnam's Sons 1977).

150 Alfred North Whitehead, *Alfred North Whitehead: An Anthology* 100 (F. S. C. Northrop and Mason W. Gross ed., Cambridge University Press 1953).

For some years now I have been concerned about the effect of our legal education on the idealism of our students. I have great faith in our students . . . they bring to the school a large measure of idealism. Do they leave with less? And if they do, is that something we can view with indifference? If they do, what is the cause? What do we do to them that makes them turn another way?[151]

Decades later, in the mid-2000s, Jenée Desmond-Harris described a similar phenomenon at a pre-graduation party. She reflected that the speeches at the party were themed around being "finally out of here" and had no reference to making a difference or feeling inspired:

The comments were saturated with distaste for HLS and the HLS experience, resentments about the graduates' commitments to work at law firms, tempered only slightly by some enthusiasm for the high salaries the coming years promised.

She contrasted this with the students she witnessed entering HLS ready to fight racism and inequality. "But suddenly, as a 2L," she quotes one student who had given in to the corporate interest firm route, "I found myself turning away from all of those open doors, questioning whether meaningful change could be made through the law, and tormented by the idea that the justice that I had always associated with the law seemed to fade in the face of politics, power, and economic analysis."[152]

So, what is the answer to Griswold's questions and Desmond-Harris' mystery? What drains our idealism? Harvard Law's own Lani Guinier has shed some light on the answer. She

151 Kahlenberg, *Broken Contract.*

152 Desmond-Harris, *"Public Interest Drift" Revisited*, 2007.

argues that when we are oriented to Harvard Law School—when we are taught to "think like a lawyer"—we actually go through two orientations. The first is the standard way we are taught to think like a lawyer: "distinguishing what is significant from what is not, working from the particular to the general and back again, and applying these habits of thought to actual human affairs."[153]

But this first lesson of "thinking like a lawyer" is paired with a second: the orientation to the professional culture—the personality, worldview, priorities and enforcement mechanisms—of the corporate interest legal field. One can identify four parts that make up this second curriculum.

Part 1: Competition as an organizing mechanism

The first part, Professor Guinier argues, is an orientation to the legal profession's culture of conflict and competition. It hones students' personalities to be more divisive and competitive. "Law," Guinier writes, "is presented as the resolution of conflict in formal settings through application of rules backed by sanctions." Problems, she continues, "are converted into binary options and they are 'resolved' by using authority and rigorous analysis to test the strength of those options."[154]

This framing of the law—which ignores mediation, legal problem-solving, and other community-minded and creative aspects of legal work—defines classroom culture. First-year classroom contributions, Guinier explains, are "an implicit competition to say the opinions professors and fellow students find smart." These opinions are "judged by their cleverness and responsiveness to the professor's chosen line of inquiry." Thus, "verbal agility"—a skill that Guinier points out is limited in legal practice mostly to "lit-

---

153 Susan Sturm & Lani Guinier, *The Law School Matrix: Reforming Legal Education in a Culture of Competition and Conformity*, 60 Vanderbilt Law Review 515 (2007).

154 *Id.*

igator[s] in adversarial trials"—is valued over cooperation and prevention.[155]

Guinier's story resonates with my experience of the first year of law school. Law school's opening weeks are completely disorienting. We never discuss the history and purpose of legal education, so we do not know exactly why we are here. We are given no guidance as to what the goal of our law school experience should be except the vague idea that we must learn to "think like a lawyer." Given no explicit purpose as guidance, most students grasp for the implicit purpose that hums around them: *you are here to win.*

Part 2: Competition becomes "The Game"

Robert Granfield, in his book *Making Elite Lawyers: Visions of Law at Harvard and Beyond,* explains the next part of this orientation, which is about the worldview that evolves out of the competition-centered personalities honed in the first unit. Granfield argues that when students start to value the competitive environment of law school more than the content discussed in that competitive environment, they develop a "detached cynicism" of seeing the law as "nothing more than a game." As students learn that professors value legal arguments more than substantive or ideological arguments and that students who hone their "detached cynicism" are treated as more intellectually sophisticated, this "game-oriented consciousness" progressively comes to replace their "justice-oriented consciousness."[156] They not only begin to lose a justice-oriented consciousness, but also begin to oppose those who hang on to it: they begin to, in Granfield's words, "disdain right-versus-wrong thinking as unprofessional and naïve."[157]

---

155 *Id.*

156 Granfield, *Making Elite Lawyers.*

157 Michael Head & Scott Mann, *Law in Perspective: Ethics, Society and Critical Thinking* 165-66 (University of New South Wales Press 2005), quoting Granfield.

Granfield is not alone in making this argument. Harvard Law's Mary Ann Glendon talks of the lawyer becoming a "virtuoso of single-mindedness—like a professional soldier or the surgeon who drapes all but the affected part of the patient under a sheet."[158] Guinier argues that this constant competition results in students losing legal imagination, which requires risk-taking, indeterminacy, and creativity—qualities which are "hard to develop when you are worrying constantly about keeping up, mastering the rules, and out-performing your competition."[159] The Class of 1977's Lynne Bernabei put it best to *Washington Monthly* a year after graduation:

> The real lesson taught by Harvard Law School is that no values are really very important. A lawyer may, with honor, represent anyone or anything. How one uses one's skills as a lawyer is insignificant since the adversary system in which everyone has an attorney guarantees that justice, somehow, will win out in the end. Harvard Law School is, above all, an apolitical place.[160]

To those who argue that this supremacy of the "game-orientation" is a quality not especially peculiar to law, Guinier puts forward the other professional schools as counterexamples. While expertise in law school is developed through individual interpretation and analysis, medical education, Guinier argues, "emphasizes 'deep understanding' and students taking responsibility over their education. Business school, meanwhile, "emphasizes 'decision-making' and 'action.'" Moreover, medical

---

158 Mary Ann Glendon, *A Nation Under Lawyers: How the Crisis in the Legal Profession Is Transforming American Society* 38 (Harvard University Press 1994).

159 Sturm & Guinier, *The Law School Matrix.*

160 Lynne Bernabei, The Case of the Co-opted Critic: Ralph Nader and Harvard Law School, *The Washington Monthly*, https://www.unz.org/Pub/WashingtonMonthly-1978oct-00051.

and business schools, she adds, focus on group learning and collaboration, assuming these to be "vital skills to the respective professions," while law schools rarely move beyond individualized learning.[161]

Granfield and Guinier's account of this part of our professional orientation squares with my law school experience. Throughout my first year, I witnessed a vague sense of competition evolve into an all-out game.

First, I watched hierarchies appear out of nowhere: people who had never heard of any law firm or student group on day one could soon name and order all of them by prestige. In a few weeks, student conversations became filled with the ins and outs of what it takes to interview into Harvard Defenders, write on the Law Review, get a coveted clerkship, be hired for a summer position at WilmerHale in D.C., or become a research assistant for a famous professor.

Second, I witnessed how discussions about the *content* of our legal education became subsumed into discussions about the competition itself. Discussions about what issues were actually addressed in a morning class became replaced by discussions about how smart a student or professor was in that class. Employment dreams themed around the *content* of legal work—"I want to fight for children"—became replaced by dreams based on the *form* of the work: "I just want to work at a place that is stimulating." As law school progresses, the interesting and prestigious triumphed over the noble and meaningful.

Third, I saw how disdain for moral thinking grew among those who became more committed to the game-oriented consciousness. Students who spoke up in class about justice-related issues started being called, at best, unrigorous, and, at worse, "self-righteous." Any discussions that echoed Nader's questions about "the just deployment of legal manpower" started being

---

161 *Id.*

considered rude in the second year of law school, because peers had already signed up for firm jobs. Arguments about the flaws of nonprofits and the futility of public interest legal work proliferated. The game may pit everyone against each other most of the time, but when the game itself is under attack, law students are more than willing to cooperate to defend their worldview.

Part 3: The winners of the game: "The Cult of Smart"

This type of personality (competitive) and worldview (game-oriented) leads us to a third part of the professional orientation: acculturation to a "cult of smart," where those with the sharpest and narrowest analytical skills are held in acclaim, regardless of their moral orientation.

The introductory rites of legal education's cult of smart occur in the first-year classroom, with student acclaim for smart professors. The first-year classroom, Guinier points out, centers all attention on the professor, with "professors fishing for the 'right' answers, and students trying to catch the hook." Professors frame the whole 'game': the questions that should be considered important, the eventual 'correct' answers to those questions, and the affirmative and negative reactions to students' guesses. Since bringing in outside morality or ideology (or even facts from the real world) into the environment is discouraged, students evaluate the entire exercise on the cleverness of their professors' analytical gymnastics. That is how, Guinier argues, being smart becomes "a value itself, detached from what people want to accomplish with their mastery."[162]

This cult of smart eventually trickles out from students' views of professors to students' views of the judges they are reading. It is not uncommon to hear classroom comments like "I might disagree, but this argument is so clever and well-written," or "Say what you want about what he advocated for, he was a

---

162 *Id.*

genius." This is reinforced by the physical school environment, which hangs pictures of academic faculty and 'genius' jurists— as opposed to clinicians and courageous reformers—most prominently on the walls.

And finally, this cult of smart eventually trickles down into student culture. The students who are best at the game of law school—those who might be the research assistants for the smartest professors, those who might be clerks on the Supreme Court—are often the object of peer fascination, with little regard given in the hallway chatter to their moral courage or to which legal interests they plan to serve after law school.

Harvard Law's Roberto Unger likes to quote Schopenhauer on this subject: *"Talent hits a target no one else can hit; genius hits a target no one else can see."* To use Schopenhauer's frame, those in the cult of smart at Harvard Law School mistake talent for genius.

Part 4: Rankings as enforcement mechanisms

To Guinier, these three layers of our professionalization— honing a competitive personality, developing a game-oriented consciousness, and holding up a cult of smart—are enforced by a final layer: the ranking system.

This begins with exams, which are focused on rank-ordering students, rather than giving meaningful feedback. It continues into the Law Review competition, which becomes an "inner ring" of the law school to demarcate the best of the best.[163] This ranking system is finalized in law school through firm and clerkship placements, which both have an acknowledged implicit hierarchy: WilmerHale, Cravath and Wachtell, the Supreme Court and D.C. Circuit at the top.

---

163 "The Inner Ring" in C.S. Lewis, *Transposition and Other Addresses* 55-66 (Geoffrey Bles 1949).

A smooth transition to corporate interest firms

This orientation provides a smooth transition to working at corporate interest law firms. As one *Harvard Law Review* note puts it: "The seeds are planted early so that later, when students start down the corporate track, the journey, although a path not actively chosen, seems natural and even inevitable."[164]

Everything syncs up. A competitive personality is rewarded at big firms, where there are constant opportunities to impress your new professors: the partners and senior associates. The game-oriented mindset is helpful to limit moral distractions caused by the actual—and sometimes disturbing—content of advancing the legal interests of the wealthy and powerful. The cult of smart still reigns as certain partners are lauded at firms for their analytical wizardry. And finally, the enforcement mechanism smoothly transitions from grades to money. Judge Patrick Schiltz, quoted by Guinier, puts it well:

> First they competed to get into a prestigious college, then they competed for college grades. Then they competed for LSAT scores. Then they competed to get into a prestigious law school. Then they competed for law school grades. Then they competed to make the law review. Then they competed for clerkships. Then they competed to get hired by a big law firm . . . They're playing a game. And money is how the score is kept in that game . . . Money is what tells them if they're more successful than the lawyer in the next office.[165]

And it is not just the winners of the law school game who are synced up to enter big firms—it is the losers, too. As Guinier points out, the "law firm flattery" given to students at receptions

---

164 *Making Docile Lawyers: An Essay on the Pacification of Law Students*, 111 Harvard Law Review 2027 (1998).

165 Sturm & Guinier, *The Law School Matrix*, quoting Judge Patrick Schiltz.

and interviews is often "essential to recovering the self-esteem they lost when they got their first-year grades."[166] After having been through this professional orientation to the second sense of how to "think like a lawyer," graduates are just happy to know there is a similar game waiting for them on the other side.

Alternatives hamstrung

As Jenée Desmond-Harris points out, this cultural conveyer belt from the first week of 1L to corporate interest legal work is not relevant to all students at Harvard Law School. A minority share of students come to law school with the intention of pursuing corporate interest work. A relatively equal-sized share of students come to law school with a deep commitment to public interest legal work and a plan for how their law school experience could support that vocation. Neither of these groups are swayed much by the attraction of corporate interest legal work: the former is already convinced and the latter is outside of its orbit. It is the group in the middle—the vast majority of Harvard Law School students that Desmond-Harris calls "justice-minded, but passive"—that this cultural force affects.

Currently, as Desmond-Harris shows, most students who are "open to" or "interested in" pursuing a social change agenda but have no clear commitment or plan eventually end up working for corporate interest firms. In the interviews Desmond-Harris conducted, you can see the difference that having an abstract civic interest versus having a concrete civic commitment makes in determining one's employment outcome. Those who eventually pursued public interest careers laid out plans and commitments to Desmond-Harris in their interviews: *"Criminal justice is what I wanted to do"*; *"I was committed to doing anti-discrimination work when I came to the law school"*; *"Meaningful civil rights work"*; *"Bridge the gap between the haves and the*

---

166 *Id.*

have-nots." In fact, Desmond notes, among the strongest predictors of whether a student would pursue public interest legal work after graduation was whether the student had a political orientation and participated in prior political activism.

On the other side, those who eventually pursued corporate interest careers gave much more vague, searching answers: *"I thought law school would give me ample opportunity to decide what kind of lawyer I wanted to become;" "I expected to get some clarity about the particular career I wanted;" "I saw law school as being able to have power;" "I definitely expected law school to help me find out what I was interested in."* Desmond-Harris discovered that most of the students who are "open to" public interest work but who expect their law school experience to provide answers as to what they concretely want to work on do indeed receive an answer from their experience: "work in corporate interest law."[167]

To provide a counterweight to the pull of corporate interest law among the "justice-minded, but passive," an affirmative, communal alternative would need to flourish. However, attempts at these alternatives are hamstrung.

First, there is a mass faculty neutrality as to the question of what is the appropriate balance of deployment of legal manpower coming out of Harvard Law School. No one wants to take sides in the great "public interest vs. corporate interest" debate and the administration actively tries to blur the lines between the two career paths. The company line is: "We are just here to help you achieve what you came here to achieve." But the reality is most students do not come here with an idea of what they plan to do. Many come here, in fact, precisely because they do not know what to do and need guidance. Our community's elders cannot step back and say they are simply helping students realize their personal goals while the environment is aggressively structuring what those goals become.

---

167 Desmond-Harris, *"Public Interest Drift" Revisited.*

Or, to put it in Howard Zinn's eloquent terms: When four times as many Harvard Law graduates are advancing the legal interests of the wealthy and powerful as are advancing the legal interests of poor and public at large, "you can't be neutral on a moving train."

One can understand why a university administration would be worried about taking specific stances on political issues. However, an administration need not do so to provide space for vocation-building. Little is done even in terms of that: as Guinier points out, the only required part of the law school curriculum that even gets close to vocation-building is "professional responsibility" courses, which narrow in on ethical quandaries and rarely address questions of the distribution of services and corporate power head on.[168] Some call young lawyers the "conscience of the profession." Unger calls students "tongue-tied prophets."[169] And yet little is done to unpack our creative visions or awaken our conscience.

Even worse, not enough community is built at the law school to bolster student-driven vocation-building. Granfield found that those students who ended up deploying their legal power to advance the interests of the poor and working class after law school remained committed throughout their three years by "associating with other students who possessed these ideals" in a "community of opposition."[170] Despite recent efforts by the Office of Public Interest Advising to foster a social-change community on campus, the vast majority of "justice-minded, but passive" students still hardly feel part of any vocational community. Community-building within first year 'sections'

168 Sturm & Guinier, *The Law School Matrix*.

169 Roberto Mangabeira Unger, *The Self Awakened: Pragmatism Unbound* 176 (Harvard University Press 2007).

170 Lynn A. Addington and Jessica L. Waters, Public Interest 101: Using the Law School Curriculum to Quell Public Interest Drift and Expand Students' Public Interest Commitment, 21 *Journal of Gender, Social Policy & the Law* 79 (2012).

rarely has a moral or vocational element to it; there is no public network of professors committed to collectively inspiring a new generation of changemakers; and the deepest community experiences among extracurriculars are cordoned off in exclusive organizations with few members, like the Law Review, the Legal Aid Bureau, and the Board of Student Advisors.

This lack of moral direction or community has led to a campus culture of insecurity, anxiety, and confusion. This is not a natural way for humans to act: we are cooperative rather than competitive; we are justice-oriented rather than game-oriented; and, deep down, we value friendship, loyalty, and courage over smarts. We know that the pursuit of ever more exclusive positions in ranking systems is a quest that, as C.S. Lewis warned in his speech about "The Inner Ring," will "break [our] hearts unless [we] break it." And yet, out of habit, we continue on this warped path.[171]

In response to our pervasive insecurity, there have been attempts to make Harvard Law "nicer"—different than the cutthroat world of Turow's *One L*. But instead of ending the game—instead of changing the root of our insecurity—the school has simply told us all that we are all winning it: *"there are enough slots among the elite for you all to fill."* As one speaker crassly told our class on orientation week: "Stop worrying. You're the heap-toppers."

The concept of "imposter syndrome" is a good example of this path. People fear that they do not deserve to be at a place like Harvard Law—that they are "imposters"—and, as a result, we respond by saying "No, you are just suffering from imposter syndrome. Of course you deserve to be here." But this ignores an alternative answer that could be given: *that no one deserves to be here; that our desert of these resources is determined by our future choices, not our past 'worth;' that if we use these resources in the*

---

171 C.S. Lewis, "The Inner Ring."

*spirit of our mission, to advance justice and societal well-being, then
we will have shown we are not imposters.*

We rarely are told that latter answer. The game plays on.

4b. A curriculum that pacifies students

This all-encompassing cultural orientation is more impactful
than any curricular program at Harvard Law School. This is why
Guinier is skeptical of curricular reform: any one-off teaching
experiment, she writes, will be marginalized or subsumed by
the underlying culture.[172] Bernabei went further in her critique
of resting reformist hopes on curricular changes:

> [Curricular reform] has been resurrected with eerie regu-
> larity every 15 or 20 years . . . Yale historian Robert Stevens
> describes the cyclical process of criticizing legal education:
> 'As all the basic arguments about curriculum reform are
> trotted out in each decade in apparently blissful ignorance
> that they have ever been discussed before, so in terms of legal
> research, the wheel is reinvented with depressing frequency.'
> The problem . . . is that law schools do not instill a sense of
> the law as a means to justice. There is no feeling in those
> classrooms that the whole point of law is that what is right
> ought to be what prevails.[173]

Nevertheless, seeing how Harvard Law's curriculum and
pedagogical methods have come to pacify students is key to understanding how we have lost sight of our public interest mission.

The Socratic method

Any curricular history of Harvard Law naturally starts with
the two innovations of Christopher Columbus Langdell, our

---

172 Sturm & Guinier, *The Law School Matrix.*

173 Bernabei, *The Case of the Co-opted Critic: Ralph Nader and Harvard Law School.*

school's most influential dean: the socratic method and the case method. These two methods, though apparently neutral, have significant political content baked into their forms.

"The Socratic method," Turow writes in *One L*, "is without question one of the things which makes legal education—particularly the first year, when Socraticism is most extensively used—distinct." He summarizes the teaching strategy as follows:

> Generally, Socratic discussion begins when a student—I'll call him Jones—is selected without warning by the professor and questioned. Traditionally, Jones will be asked to 'state the case,' that is, to provide an oral rendition of the information normally contained in a case brief. Once Jones has responded, the professor—as Socrates did with his students—will question Jones about what he has said, pressing him to make his answers clearer. If Jones says that the judge found that the contract had been breached, the professor will ask what specific provision of the contract had been violated and in what manner. The discussion will proceed that way, with the issues narrowing. At some point, Jones may be unable to answer. The professor can either select another student at random, or—more commonly—call on those who've raised their hands. The substitutes may continue the discussion of the case with the professor, or simply answer what Jones could not, the professor than resuming his interrogation of Jones.[174]

This method has its benefits: it keeps every student alert during class; it is an alternative to lecture for large class sizes, bringing in multiple voices into the conversation; and it sharpens students' analytical agility. However, a variety of critiques, some of which were already being voiced at Turow's

---

174 Turow, *One L*.

time in law school, have spotlighted the throughline between Socraticism and our culture of civic complacency.

First, as Harvard Law's own Duncan Kennedy has argued, the socratic method is "hierarchical with a vengeance."[175] The multiple voices heard during a socratic class session make it appear to be a more participatory form of teaching than, say, a lecture. But, as Kennedy points out, students have autonomy during a lecture: the teacher can drone on, but the students have the freedom to think about what they want to think about during class. Plus, if lecture is paired with a discussion period, students have space to launch critiques of and propose alternatives to a lecturer's line of thinking. In the socratic method, every student is always on edge, in constant preparation for providing the answers that the professor wants to hear. No room is left for critical questioning.

Second, the socratic method is intellectually pacifying. Sure, the method is rigorous: students must be quick on their feet to provide the facts of a case, the reasons a judge might have ruled the way she did, and the broader implications of such decisions. But intellectual vigor, unlike analytical rigor, is about, as Nader put it once, "forming and stimulating" the important questions and conversations, rather than repeating and identifying the right fact-patterns and answers.[176]

Third, the socratic method often naturalizes the past. A classic socratic question is *Why do you think this rule is set up this way?* Answers to that question are often framed in a way that assumes the judge's rule to be the most natural and necessary way for things to be organized. Answers that bring in historic contexts—say, "it is set up that way because that would benefit the judge and people similar to him," "it is set up that

---

175 Duncan Kennedy, Legal Education and the Reproduction of Hierarchy, 32 *Journal of Legal Education* 591 (1982).

176 Nader, *The Ralph Nader Reader*, at 389.

way because the judge lacks institutional imagination," or "it is set up that way because one party lacked high-powered lawyers and lobbyists"—are few and far between. The more historicized question of *"Why do you think this rule wound up this way?"* is rarely proffered during a socratic session.

Fourth, the socratic method alone leaves little room for legal imagination. As Guinier defines it, "legal imagination is a form of 'thinking like a lawyer' that enables its practitioners to produce a more robust definition of the problem at hand, and a more plural version of possible solutions."[177] It is about, in the words of Minow and fellow Harvard Law professor Todd Rakoff, "the ability to generate the multiple characterizations, multiple versions, multiple pathways, [and] multiple solutions" to which they can then apply their "very well-honed analytic skills."[178] If the de-naturalizing question is *"Why do you think this rule wound up this way?"* then the imagination-sparking question is *"What are some ways this rule could be different?"* Though both questions are key to building civic competency, neither are commonplace in socratic classrooms.

The case method

In first-year law school courses, and in all subsequent 'black letter law' courses, the socratic method is paired with the case method: the process of learning the law by reading judicial opinions in appellate cases. In instituting the case method, Langdell's hope was that students, in reading and parsing appellate decisions, would induce the core principles and doctrines of the law. This method, as David A. Garvin explains in a 2003 *Harvard Magazine* profile on Langdell's pedagogy, "shifted the locus of learning from law offices to the library." Thanks to Langdell,

---

177 Sturm & Guinier, *The Law School Matrix.*

178 Todd D. Rakoff & Martha Minow, A Case for Another Case Method, 60 *Journal of Legal Education* 597 (2007).

developing "craft skills and hands-on experience" became less central to a legal education than the "mastery of principles." Langdell said so himself: "What qualifies a person ... to teach law is not experience in the work of a lawyer's office ... not experience in the trial or argument of cases ... but experience in learning law."[179]

Unfortunately, this designed-in severance of legal education from the real world of legal experience has often cursed the case method with the same pacifying tendencies of its socratic twin. The case method teaches the law as if it exists outside of time: outside of historical context, outside of future possibility, and outside of present reality.

In the text of appellate decisions, there is hardly any information shared about the history of how certain legal principles came to be. As Kennedy has explained, students are left to assume that there is a rational explanation behind each judicial decision they read. They are tasked with the sole challenge of finding this explanation. The cases themselves, and the legal principles one is to induce from the cases, are treated like universal principles of nature, rather than what they actually are: historical, political decisions made by flawed individuals with specific political identities, experiences, and interests. When historical, political documents like appellate decisions are naturalized into timeless principles through the case method, present students can be miseducated and disempowered. They can be implicitly taught that the legal structures they inhabit are natural and necessary, rather than imperfect, political, and susceptible to reimagination.

It is in this way that the absence of historical context in the case method can limit future imagination as well. As Seligman explains in the *High Citadel*:

---

179 David A. Garvin, Making the Case, *Harvard Magazine* (2003), http://harvardmagazine.com/2003/09/making-the-case-html.

> By insisting that the appropriate knowledge of a field of law
> could be abstracted from a set of leading cases, the early case-
> book authors denied students the opportunity to engage in
> the more speculative study of what *should* be the ends of law
> and under what circumstances should the premises of judges
> be questioned.[180]

If one is solely focused on understanding the allegedly rational and universal thought processes of a particular judge, there is little room for imagining an alternative path forward for the law. As Langdell wished, the case method may invite students to be "scientists" discovering how the law works. But it does not invite them to be engineers capable of imagining new theories informed by this alleged science.

The present, like the past and the future, is also absent from the case method. When reading appellate decisions, students learn nothing of the greater context of the case: the political atmosphere at the time, the imbalance of power between each party's lawyers, and the institutions—like police and prisons, corporations and unions, and even the bar and the bench them-selves—that structured the facts of the case. Appellate decisions do not reveal the way the law affects society outside of the court-room, such as when the law prevents things from happening or when the law informs the design of non-legal institutions, like hospitals and schools. By its very nature, the case method is unable to educate students on the endemic lawlessness in American society: the rights never vindicated in court due to lack of government enforcement, underfunded public interest advocacy groups, understaffed civil legal aid offices, and efforts by corporate interests to limit the use of tort and contract law through mandatory arbitration and boilerplate forms.

Most conspicuously absent from Harvard Law's case-heavy

---

180 Seligman, *The High Citadel.*

curriculum is the study of corporate interest law firms. As documented in works such as Nader and Wesley J. Smith's *No Contest: Corporate Lawyers and the Perversion of Justice in America* and Mark Green's *The Other Government: The Unseen Power of Washington Lawyers*, America's corporate interest law firms are among the most powerful private organizations in American law, politics, and culture. Their immense influence extends beyond courtrooms to regulatory agencies, Congress, the American Bar Association, and corporate culture. Some have been agents of the opposition in many of American history's most lauded advancements in justice. And yet, the average 1L at Harvard Law School is rarely invited to examine with a critical and scholarly eye these private titans of our present legal system.

Finally, the case method educationally pales in comparison to actually visiting the venues of the justice system, like courts, prisons, police stations, border detention centers, public defender offices, and civil legal aid waiting rooms. Indeed, the case method may help students think like certain types of *attorneys*—advocates for specific clients—but its empirical starvation prevents it from being sufficient to teach students to think like *lawyers*: members and caretakers of the legal profession, tasked with servicing the justice system and advancing its public interest mission.

The reform movements

Fortunately, throughout the past century, there have been multiple reform efforts targeted at Langdell's stultifying curriculum.

First came the Legal Realists, who argued for more practical legal education, trumpeting Holmes' message that the life of the law is not logic, but experience. Early twentieth-century legal philosopher Jerome Frank took on Langdell's legacy, arguing that "something of immense worth was lost when our leading law schools wholly abandoned the legal apprentice system." To regain what was lost and introduce students to the reality of the legal system beyond appellate decisions, he proposed first, that case books should include the complete record of cases, including original filings and trial transcripts; second, that students and their teachers should make frequent visits to trial and appellate courts; and third, that legal clinics should be established to supervise students in providing services to law offices, governmental agencies, and legislative committees. It is through these brushes with the real world, Frank and other Realists hoped, that legal education would introduce students to a view of law that, in Holmes' words, "finds its philosophy not in self-consistency ... but in history and the nature of human needs."[181]

Decades later, Kennedy would echo the Realists' critique, decrying how law school teaches legal skills "in isolation from actual lawyering experience." He went one step further than his early century counterparts, though, arguing that this separation of "legal reasoning" from legal practice helps explain the dominance of corporate interest firm employment at schools like Harvard Law. To Kennedy, this lack of exposure to legal practice "disables students from any future role but that of apprentice in a law firm organized in the same manner as a law school, with older lawyers controlling the content and pace of depoliticized craft training in a setting of intense competition and no feedback."[182] To Frank and the Realists—and Kennedy and the neo-Realists—civic-minded legal work requires a practical understanding of the realities of the legal system. Unequipped by their law school education, most graduates feel more comfortable with the lax standards of the large corporate interest

---

181 *Id.*

182 Kennedy, *Legal Education and the Reproduction of Hierarchy.*

firms that do not require, and may even prefer, that their new recruits do not have much practical experience.

Another major reform effort came with the 1947 Curriculum Committee report, authored by Professor Lon L. Fuller, which argued that the law should cease to be taught in isolation of related social sciences. Legal training, the committee wrote, "does not give the student a philosophic or historic grounding in the law or an understanding of the broader functions of the legal profession." Students should learn of "empirical studies of the consequences of important national laws." and "the problems of planning and strategy [with] which lawyers are chiefly concerned in practice."[183] Decades later, Kennedy would, like he did with the Realists and their case for experiential learning, re-articulate the Fuller Committee's case for teaching social sciences with his own critical take, arguing that learning legal philosophy and history is necessary to develop a "theoretically critical attitude" toward the legal system. Without it, students "just don't know enough to figure out where the teacher is fudging, misrepresenting, and otherwise distorting legal thinking and legal reality."[184]

The most recent curricular reform initiative came with the efforts by Minow and Rakoff to integrate the stimulation of legal imagination into Harvard Law's curriculum. In 2004, Rakoff, Minow, and others commenced a major curricular review to better align the Harvard Law curriculum with the complexities and challenges of the new century. In 2007, they published some of their findings in a frank *Vanderbilt Law Review* article, arguing that Langdell's case method fails in its mission to teach students "how to think like a lawyer." They question both Langdell's decision to deem the appellate court "the paradigmatic institutional setting for thinking about a legal

---

183 Seligman, *The High Citadel.*

184 Kennedy, *Legal Education and the Reproduction of Hierarchy.*

problem" and his faith that legal "Truth" can be discovered by students in a scientific way. To Rakoff and Minow, Langdell's idea that "what constitutes a true lawyer" is being able to apply doctrines "with constant facility and certainty to the ever-tangled skein of human affairs" is anachronistic. "Lawyering," the two professors contend, "is more creative and less determinate" than Langdell formulates.

In examining how to implement their new conception of what skills should be fostered in a legal education, Rakoff and Minow turn toward other professional schools' alternative conception of the case method. The cases discussed in business, public policy, and even medical schools consist "of much more information and a much more open-ended situation, than the appellate cases used in law schools." As a result, Rakoff and Minow explain, "business school students ... generate alternative solutions and choose among them more ably than the typical law student" and "medical school students more successfully learn to identify what they do not know and how to find it out."

Rakoff and Minow conclude their article with a rousing call for legal imagination:

> In our view, what we have called 'legal imagination' is every bit as much a part of thinking like a lawyer as are the analytical skills we already teach. Truly, it is hard to ask students to start learning to move about the whole legal structure when they have only just learned the location of the rooms and the names of the furniture. But we think the greater fear is that, if we do not make the effort to challenge students in this way, students will learn to think of the legal system as only so many rooms, so many pieces of furniture, that they can never reorder. ... [O]ur society is full of new problems demanding new solutions, and less so than in the past are

lawyers inventing these solutions. We think we can, and ought to, do better.[185]

In a way, Rakoff and Minow had mainstreamed part of the once-radical critiques of Guinier and Kennedy: law students might learn how to answer their professors' narrow socratic questions, but they rarely learn how to ask the right, critical questions, nor develop the confidence to reform or re-imagine the legal system.

The Great Compromise: "let them eat electives!"

Most reform efforts throughout Harvard's second century followed a similar pattern: first, reformers would launch a critique of Langdell's curriculum; second, as the reform effort gained a following, tensions would rise between the progressive reformers and a recalcitrant old guard; and finally, a compromise would be struck in which, to appease the old guard, the first-year curriculum would be left relatively unchanged, and, to appease the reformers, new second- and third-year electives would be added.

One might call this great curricular compromise the "let them eat electives!" approach. The Realists would eventually be appeased with functional electives on labor, corporations, the family, cities and, eventually, television and the internet. The Fuller Committee's efforts would eventually result in a potpourri of electives featuring the various academic specialties, such as the sociology of law, law and economics, philosophy of law, and law and psychology.[186] The movements of the 1960s and 70s were responded to with even more electives: civil rights law, environmental law, feminist legal theory, disability law, and more.

---

185 Rakoff & Minow, A Case for Another Case Method.
186 Seligman, *The High Citadel*.

Pairing an anti-poverty agenda with a desire for more hands-on legal education, Bellow reinvigorated Harvard Law's clinical programs. Today, to the school's immense credit, there are 18 in-house clinics at Harvard Law. However, the clinical opportunities established by Bellow and others, as expected under the compromise, have slotted in as electives, unintegrated with the mandatory first-year curriculum. Bellow himself felt the "clinics as one-off elective" system was not enough, going as far as to found an integrated clinical institute in 1977. He later recounted how he explained his thinking to Dean Albert Sacks:

> I say, "Well I think the thing that's most needed are legal services schools." I mean, institutions that will bridge the gap between the absence of training and legal services offices for new people. And the law school's research that touches none of the theoretical and policy issues that you need to deal with to do something about poverty ... And Al Sacks took that to the Harvard faculty and the Harvard faculty voted unanimously to support a 25-person institute in which every single course was taught at site ... So we had the entire third year in which clinical work and classroom work was integrated.[187]

(Before this moment, clinical education has faced resistance throughout Harvard Law's history. Dean Griswold had said he hoped the school "won't go overboard on clinical legal education." When the Harvard Legal Aid Bureau was established, a Harvard alumni newsletter assured readers that students would "sacrifice ... comparatively little time" for the effort. In the same newsletter, it was noted with pride that students who

---

187 Zona Hostetler & Gary Bellow, Interview with Gary Bellow at National Equal Justice Library Oral History Collection, Georgetown Law Library, March 17, 1999, https://repository.library.georgetown.edu/bitstream/handle/10822/709332/nejl009_g_bellow.pdf?sequence=3.

were members of the Massachusetts militia were excused from exams to serve in the suppression of a textile workers' strike.[188])

The "problem-solving workshop," Minow and Rakoff's attempt to create a more imaginative case method, is one of the few reform proposals to actually break into the mandatory first-year curriculum. But the course's fate is revealing: it lasts only three weeks, is graded pass-fail, and is dismissed by many students as a box to check. (Worse over, the course, held during the winter term, is punctuated by evenings spent drinking at free receptions held at the priciest Cambridge bars and sponsored by major corporate interest firms.)

The result of the compromise is that there is no clear and unified theory of what law school aims to achieve. Students experience law school as the bizarre mix of a first-year of aggressive competition over who can best master a nineteenth-century curriculum followed by two years of random electives. What Seligman wrote in 1978 is still true today:

> At Harvard, and at most other leading law schools, no introductory course clearly explains to students how the American legal system, in fact, works; what are its underlying theoretical ideas; how the system developed historically; what are its most important enduring controversies.[189]

There have been attempts to unify the law school experience. In the 1950s, Harvard Law professors Henry Hart and Albert Sacks proposed the "problem method" as a way to unify legal education around real-world problem-solving. Students were to be presented with a series of problems and asked to discuss how private individuals, courts, legislatures, and government

---

188 Seligman, *The High Citadel.*
189 *Id.*

agencies would resolve those problems. Students, they hoped, would be concerned with a central question: "What should be the political relationship among private individuals, courts, legislatures, and agencies in a democratic legal system?"[190]

In 1959, a university committee on the future of legal education decried Harvard Law's failure to convey "a sense of evolution and movement of law." No course, the committee explained, addressed the function of lawyers in society, the purposes of the law, and the way the law could embody and accomplish society's values and objectives. In response, they proposed a "perspective" course to present law through a historic lens. Out of the report came a new mandatory first-year course, "Development of Legal Institutions."

However, by 1968, Development of Legal Institutions had ceased to be a required course. The loss of such a course was immediately felt: In October 1974, a group of students mounted a protest over having "never been told of any of the problems related to the distribution of legal services" during their time in law school. The students' protest would be unsuccessful: 1968 would be the last year that Harvard Law would have anything close to a theoretical orientation within its first-year curriculum.[191]

The curriculum's complicity

This curriculum—which lacks a unified framework and has responded to foundational critiques solely by piling on second- and third-year electives—is complicit in Harvard Law's public interest crisis.

The "let them eat electives" approach to curricular reform never reaches the most impressionable students: first-years. As a result, while their second- and third-year counterparts

---

190 *Id.*
191 *Id.*

are experiencing a course of study informed by a century of progress in legal, cultural, and pedagogical thought, first-year students might as well be attending law school in the nineteenth century. This anachronistic orientation to the law colors the rest of law school, framing how all future courses should be processed. As Rakoff and Minow put it: "The template for legal thinking established in the first year of law school has real staying power."[192]

Guinier has described how the first-year curriculum trains students in what is the "core" and "periphery" of law:

> The structure of courses in the first semester of the first year of law school, combined with the law firm culture conveyed by upper-class students, constructs for students a definition of what is real law, as opposed to what is 'mere' policy. This structure conveys the impression that appellate litigation and corporate practice constitute law's core, and that law emerges when judicial actors interpret the arguments of lawyers, the policies of legislators, or the decision of administrators.[193]

As a result, Guinier writes, the second- and third-year electives that might open students up to the history, theory, present context, or future possibilities of the law are marginalized. No matter how many elective courses express alternative ideas, any course diverging from what Guinier calls the first-year "operating system"—"a theory of law (cognitive and objective), a concept of professionalism (adversarial and neutral) and a view of education (competitive and uniform)"—are considered soft and peripheral.[194]

This resonates with my experience of the transition between my class' first and second year of Harvard Law School. What is

---

192 Rakoff & Minow, *A Case for Another Case Method.*

193 Sturm & Guinier, The Law School Matrix.

194 *Id.*

deemed mandatory and voluntary by the administration shapes students' views of what is important. When taking a torts course is mandatory and participating in a student practice organization is voluntary, students view learning black letter law as more important to their legal education than participating in hands-on legal service. When civil procedure courses are mandatory and clinics are voluntary, students view clinical experience as a "nice-to-have" rather than a "must-have." Graduating from Harvard Law School without knowing about, say, promissory estoppel is considered a gap in one's legal education, while graduating without having visited a housing court or knowing about the debate between the legal realists and idealists is not. The core and periphery is set by the end of the first year.

Unfortunately, most students only have the first-year curriculum to inform their understanding of the law before determining their post-graduation plans. The Early Interview Program, the school-sponsored recruitment program where most students are paired with their post-graduation employer, is held in the August after the students' first year, before the modern electives of the second and third year can even be experienced. This means that no matter how many forward-thinking and civic-minded electives are piled into the second and third years of the law school curriculum, the relationship between the curriculum and student employment choices still hinges on the regressive first-year curriculum.

A modernized first-year curriculum with a unified framework might be able to address these problems. However, the current first-year curriculum, as it stands, leaves students in a fog. Sadly, the reflections of 1930s Harvard Law student David Riesman on the first-year experience still hold true today:

> Most first-year students ... fail to see the woods for the trees when thrown into five case courses without an understanding of

what the system means or what its objectives are. Indeed, they graduate with very little understanding of the development of the law, of its main figures, of its more general concepts.[195]

Kennedy, a half a century later, echoed Riesman:

The materials present every legal issue as distinct from every other, as a tub on its own bottom, so to speak, with no hope or even any reason to hope that from law study one might derive an integrating vision of what law is, how it works, or how it might changed.[196]

First-year students, Kennedy writes, have no way to think about law "in a way that will allow one to enter into it, to criticize without utterly rejecting it, and to manipulate it without self-abandonment to their system of thinking and doing." Students are immediately required to learn the "foreign language" of the law and told that "their success or failure largely turns on swiftly learning to use the new language," leaving no time to find the political substance of the rules they are studying.[197]

I once brought up this fog with then-Dean Minow, sharing with her that I was worried first-year students were lost without learning the history, theory, and creative potential of the law. She insisted that each professor would handle it in each individual course. This never occurred in my first year. As Minow had insisted in her own pedagogical reform efforts ten years before, if there is no serious effort from administrators to institute and empower curricular alternatives in the first year, the dominant, nineteenth-century model will push any fresh method to the periphery.

---

195 Seligman, The High Citadel.

196 Kennedy, Legal Education and the Reproduction of Hierarchy.

197 Id.

With first years left in a fog of black-letter details and second- and third-years viewing the electives that could better orient them as peripheral 'add-ons,' the Harvard Law curriculum as a whole fails to light a spark inside the students who Desmond-Harris calls "justice-minded but passive." As Desmond-Harris explains, such students, who make up a majority of the Harvard Law student body, "ultimately choose large law firm employment because their interest in and openness to social change careers are not harnessed" during their first year.

The interview Desmond-Harris conducted with firm-going students support her case. One first year student who was going to a corporate interest law firm in the upcoming summer told Desmond-Harris: "I haven't really learned anything about the operation of the legal system that has influenced my plans so far." Another student heading to a firm shared: "I thought law school would involve more critiquing the current system and thinking of ways to improve it . . . and I don't think we do much of that in law school." Another: "I haven't been really inspired by anything like I thought I would be."[198]

When the curriculum fails to inform students about the operation of the legal system, influence career plans, constructively criticize the law, or even just inspire, the justice-minded but passive majority of Harvard Law students are left with nothing to counterbalance the immense pull of corporate interest recruitment.

4c. A career-building system that nudges toward corporate law

One could imagine the career system at Harvard Law serving to counterbalance the corporate interest push of the school's culture and curriculum. It could be a thumb on the scale encouraging students to contribute, as our mission state-

---

198 Desmond-Harris, *"Public Interest Drift" Revisited.*

ment impels, "to the advancement of justice and the well-being of society." Unfortunately, though, the career system nudges students even further toward corporate interest legal careers.

Such nudges are sometimes explicit, but they are most often embedded in what Harvard Law professor Cass Sunstein would call the implicit "choice architecture" of the school's career-building culture. A decision's choice architecture, as explained by Sunstein, is the design of how options are presented: design that, more often than we think, nudges choosers toward certain options. For example, if a "choice architect" places nutritious foods at eye level, grocery store shoppers are nudged toward selecting them. If you have to uncheck a donation box to opt out of donating, you are more likely to donate.[199]

These examples show what is perhaps the most powerful tool in the toolkit of a "choice architect": setting a choice's "default option." We are significantly more likely to choose options that are presented as the default and thus less likely to choose options that require active steps to be selected. *Why?* First, deference: we interpret defaults as expert recommendations. Second, loss aversion: we feel that switching options is 'losing' the default option and thus are subconsciously averse to 'losing' something we 'own.' Finally, inertia: we simply do not want to exert the effort to switch options. This is how free and open choices can still nudge us toward a preferred option: our subconscious deference, loss aversion, and inertia conspire to push us in a given direction.

From day one, Harvard Law's career-building system socializes students to see corporate-interest work as their default career option. This system operates in four key ways: first, corporate interest work is genericized; second, participation in corporate-interest recruiting is presumed; third, the public

---

199 Richard H. Thaler & Cass R. Sunstein, *Nudge: Improving Decisions About Health, Wealth, and Happiness* (Yale University Press 2008).

interest career office must continually fight for support; and, finally, the moral argument against corporate interest employment is quieted.

Genericizing corporate interest work

The setting of the default option of corporate interest careers begins with the language: generic language is used for corporate interest work while particular language is used for public interest work. The office tasked with public interest career advising is given a special name, "The Bernard Koteen Office of Public Interest Advising," while the office primarily tasked with corporate interest career advising is called simply the "Office of Career Services." Similarly, the recruiting program for corporate interest employers is given the generic name "Early Interview Program" (EIP), while the same program for public interest employers is given the special name "Public Interest Interview Program" (PIIP).

One could, say, imagine the advising office and interview program for public interest, government, and academic careers being called the "Office of Career Services" and the "Legal Interview Program," while the office and interview program for big firm careers being called, say, the "Office of Corporate Interest Advising" and the "Corporate Interest Interview Program."

This choice of language fits snugly with how our careers are discussed during class. Interactive hypotheticals in first-year courses tend to involve students being asked to advise their firm's "senior partner," as opposed to, say, their Department of Justice or ACLU supervisor. In my own first year, in our federal regulation hypotheticals, we were asked to imagine ourselves as a corporate interest lobbyist, rather than as, say, a public interest activist. When a defense attorney was brought in to speak to our first-year section, it was a white collar defense attorney who bragged about how he could instruct six young associates to work all night long to be ready for a client meeting. (Compare that to public defense's "meet 'em, greet 'em, and plead 'em"!) There was only one required field trip during my entire time at law school: at the end of the Problem Solving Workshop, to Foley Hoag, a corporate interest law firm.

This corporate interest shop talk during class is not new. Samuel Bleicher of the Class of 1966 had a similar experience to mine:

> Almost from the moment he walks into his first class, the HLS student is exposed to and encouraged to think in terms of Wall Street corporate-law practice. His professors talk about multi-million dollar cases they handled, his casebooks are filled with familiar business names, and his friends discuss at length the relative merit of 75- versus 125- man firms. Those who say they are going 'back home' to practice feel defensive and are presumed to have some ulterior motive, such as political aspirations. The large-firm lawyer is held out as the ideal career type. The effect of this one-sided presentation of the lawyer's alternatives is subtly to coerce many students into social, psychological, and political conformity with the image of the "successful lawyer"—the partner in a big firm.[200]

Presuming corporate interest recruitment participation

At the end of the first year summer, participation in Harvard Law's major corporate interest recruiting event, EIP, is often presented not as one of many options for students, but rather as an implicit administrative request.

First, posters flood the school. At the end of my first year, an EIP "orientation and market mixer" explicitly said "all 1Ls are strongly encouraged to attend." The same "strong encour-

---

200 Seligman, *The High Citadel.*

agement" is not present on posters for civic-minded programs like Student Practice Organizations, clinics and public interest career orientations.

Second, emails sent to students to sign up for EIP are designed to be perceived as official administrative emails aimed at everyone—similar to ones that remind you to register for courses or to sign up for on-campus housing—rather than as emails presenting specific career or extracurricular opportunities applicable to certain groups of students. At the end of my first year, for example, I received an email addressed to the entire class that, instead of, say, beginning with "if you are interested in corporate interest legal careers, we are here to help," began with: "Before you leave Cambridge for your summer jobs, we had some quick reminders in anticipation of EIP." Instead of saying "for those interested in EIP, here is the EIP web page," it said: "Bookmark our EIP webpage . . . this page includes key dates and resources for EIP prep." No similar school-wide email instructed everyone to begin preparation for public interest career interviews. Those are reserved for interested students.[201]

Worse over, when public-minded students ignore these emails, they are personally pursued by the administration. In my first year, every 1L who had not expressed interest in participating in EIP received the following email from the Office of Career Services:

Subject Line: Checking in about EIP Orientation

Hi there—I am writing because you are on a list of students who have not yet RSVP'd for the EIP Orientation and Market Mixer event which takes place this Wednesday, March 9, from 5:00—8:00 p.m. in Milstein. If you plan to participate in the Early

---

201 Email to author.

Corporate interest nudges

ocs@law.harvard.edu   4/28/16
to pedavis

To the Class of 2018:

Congratulations on completing your 1L classes! Before you leave Cambridge for your summer jobs, we had some quick reminders in anticipation of EIP:

• Notify us of your 2016 summer job by completing the Summer Employment Survey in CSM – this will take just a minute of your time.

• Sign up for the Summer Mock Interview Program by Monday, May 2. We will connect you with an attorney in the city where you will be working for a mock interview. There are two ways to sign up: through the CSM Symplicity Summer Employment Survey, or here.

• Check your in-box to confirm that you are receiving automatic email notices of our Hire Ground blog posts (the last post was sent on Thursday, April 21), so that you will not miss any time-sensitive EIP information this summer.

• Bookmark our EIP webpage: www.law.harvard.edu/eip- this page includes key dates and resources for EIP prep.

If you have any questions, please email ocs@law.harvard.edu. Our office will be open all summer for in-person, phone, and Skype appointments and we look forward to assisting you with your upcoming job search.

We wish you all the best of luck for final exams and a great summer!

–The Office of Career Services

Interview Program (EIP) in August, then I highly encourage you to attend this program which will address important information about preparing for EIP over the coming months. This will be the last program about EIP before August. Additionally, you will be able to meet a lot of employers from the specific markets in which you are interested. It's actually a lot of fun and there will be tons of food.

I know that some students have classes that evening. However, even if that is the case, I'm encouraging you to attend after classes end. If you are going to be late, please just let us know.

To RSVP click HERE. If you are going to be late, in addition to RSVP'ing, please reply to this email letting us know that you will be there after your class ends.

I hope to see you on Wednesday.[202]

Even more than the previous email, this email resembled an official administrative request. In saying that students uninterested in legal work serving corporate interests were on a "list of

---

202 Email to author.

students"who had failed to complete a task that the administration was tracking, the email embodies the exact "default option"-setting mentioned above: it implies—like the generic language used for corporate interest career-building, the in-class hypotheticals, and the Problem Solving Workshop field trip—that corporate interest legal work is the presumptive career choice for Harvard Law School students. Again, no such email was sent to, say, all the students who had not signed up for public interest career recruitment.

Even preferencing on the online bidding system for recruiting interviews shows a bias toward corporate interest careers. The pre-selected "session" in the drop-down menu is "EIP 2017 On-Campus Interviews." One has to click in and scroll past "EIP 2017 Resume Collection" to select Public Interest Interview Program recruiting. Indeed, sometimes corporate interest career-building is even *literally* the default option.

Session

✓ EIP 2017 On-Campus Interviews
PIIP 2017 On-Campus Interviews
PIIP 2017 Resume Collections
FIP 2017 Private Sector On-Campus Interviews
FIP 2017 Private Sector Resume Collections
2017 Resume Book Program

Finally, even if there were no aggressive promotion of EIP, the disparity in simplicity, certainty, and ease between corporate interest recruitment and public interest recruitment would still grease the wheels of Harvard Law's rampant corporate interest careerism. The five-day, one-off corporate interest recruiting program—consisting of more than 10,000 interviews, preceded by months of preparation at decadent firm-sponsored receptions, and producing near-complete career certainty after only one year of law school—has a gravitational pull. Even students who were not interested in such work are sucked up by it, worried about losing opportunities: "Pretty much all my friends were participating," one civic-minded student told *The Harvard Crimson* in 2012. "I think I ultimately felt like I didn't want to close any doors."[203] One can see how the psychology of choice architecture works its magic: having been told repeatedly that acceptance into Harvard Law School guarantees you a corporate interest legal career, students become "loss averse" to giving up that default option.

The Office of Career Services admits to this all-too-common story: in 2016, its director told *Harvard Magazine* that "the path of least resistance will put you at a firm in New York."[204]

This is an example of the well-documented "funnel effect" seen at prominent schools: the phenomenon where people apply to prominent schools so as to expand their options, but end up, in fact, limiting their options. *What accounts for this?* Researchers proffer two explanations: first, students who are accepted into prominent schools feel they must "live up to their degree" in the eyes of their support network and thus are averse to taking average-paying or "mid-status" jobs; and second, students become so used to jumping through standardized, institutionalized hoops that they fear leaving that routine to take a less-standard, less-institutionalized path.[205]

I will put forth a third reason, specific to our Millennial generation. The sociologist Zygmunt Bauman has described the time we are living in as one of "liquid modernity," defined by an

203 Juliet R. Bailin, At HLS, a Tough Path to Public Interest, *The Harvard Crimson*, October 29, 2012, http://www.thecrimson.com/article/2012/10/29/hls-public-service/.

204 Marina N. Bolotnikova, The Purpose of Harvard Law School, *Harvard Magazine*, August 17, 2016, http://harvardmagazine.com/2016/08/the-purpose-of-harvard-law-school.

205 Lynn Barendsen, Wendy Fischman, & Margot Locker, *The Funnel Effect: How Elite College Culture Narrows Students' Perceptions of Post-Collegiate Career Opportunities*, GoodWork ® *Project Report Series*, http://www.issuelab.org/resource/the_funnel_effect_how_elite_college_culture_narrows_students_perceptions_of_post_collegiate_career_opportunities.

overriding desire to "keep our options open" and never commit to anything for too long.[206] The corporate interest recruiters play on this Millennial fear of closing doors, setting up a system where people can just "try it out." This is often how students view the high salaries provided by corporate interest firms: not as a luxury, but as a ticket to keep their doors open. But what really happens is that doors close. For most of the "justice-minded, but passive," this path of "just trying out" EIP turns into "just trying out" corporate interest work for the summer, which turns into "just trying out" corporate interest work after graduation, which, as shown in the aforementioned career trajectory data, turns into "just trying out" corporate interest work for life. It all reminds me of an old, grim *New Yorker* cartoon: in it, simply, a gravestone carrying the epitaph "He kept his options open."

The public interest career office's fight for parity

Meanwhile, building up a system to support alternatives to this path of least resistance has been an uphill battle.

Up through the 1980s, public interest career advising at Harvard Law School consisted of, according to student accounts, filing cabinets of "outdated materials," a "long-distance phone you could use to set up interviews," and, eventually, a single part-time, under-resourced public interest advisor. It was no wonder that only about 25 students each year were accepting public interest jobs upon graduation.[207]

Fortunately, by the early 1990s, this began to change. Ironically, it was an administration attack on public interest career advising that served as the catalyst for reform. In 1989, Harvard Law corporations professor Robert C. Clark became dean. Six months into his tenure, he eliminated all public interest career

---

206 See Zygmunt Bauman, *Liquid Modernity* (Polity Press 2000).

207 Susan Dominus, A Private Battle for Public Service, 1997 *The American Lawyer* (1997).

advising positions, citing cost concerns and arguing that the positions served only "symbolic, guilt-alleviating purposes."[208]

The student body erupted in opposition to the cuts. Activists in the Classes of 1990 and 1991—including many students who would go on to become prominent public interest lawyers, like Public Citizen chair Jason Adkins and Global Trade Watch director Lori Wallach—wrote letters, circulated petitions, held rallies, hosted press conferences with supportive professors, and even printed T-shirts emblazoned with "guilt-alleviating" on the front. Their "Emergency Coalition for Public Interest Placement" (ECPIP) made national news and eventually forced the administration to form a Student-Faculty Committee to look into public interest advising, clinical programs, and even admissions at Harvard Law. Soon an offshoot campaign, inspired by their success, emerged to demand mandatory pro bono requirements for law students. Several ECPIP leaders brought the issue national and were eventually successful at spreading such requirements to law schools across the country, including Harvard Law.[209]

These years of heightened public interest activism resulted in a complete change of course for the administration. It began with the re-instatement of a public interest advisor position and the hiring of Stacy DeBroff to fill the role. DeBroff soon became a trailblazing force, eventually coming to be seen by many as the figure who, along with her eventual successor Alexa Shabecoff, elevated public interest advising, in the words of University of Virginia School of Law assistant dean of public service Kimberly Emery, "to a new level of respectability at law schools."[210]

---

208 Philip Lee, The Griswold 9 and Student Activism for Faculty Diversity at Harvard Law School in the Early 1990s, 27 *Harvard Journal of Racial & Ethnic Justice* (2011), https://scholar.harvard.edu/files/philip_lee/files/griswold_9_article_27_harv._j._racial__ethnic_just.pdf.

209 Interviews with Emergency Coalition for Public Interest Placement members.

210 Susan Dominus, A Private Battle for Public Service, *The American Lawyer.*

When she began at Harvard Law, DeBroff had witnessed how public interest students had been marginalized at the Office of Career Services. At the beginning of her tenure, civic-minded students had reported three-week waits for an appointment and DeBroff was forced to see students nonstop from eight in the morning to eight at night.

DeBroff fought back, tasking herself with the mission of figuring out how to persuade students "to hold on to their values." Backed by a student-driven campaign, she immediately lobbied for an independent public interest office that would not report nor share a budget with the larger career office. She coupled this effort with the creation of a Public Interest Job Search Guide, a book that, in the words of journalist Susan Dominus in an *American Lawyer* profile on DeBroff, "clear-cut a path for students who would otherwise have had to stumble their way through a maze of word-of-mouth connections and clues."[211]

In 1999, when Shabecoff succeeded DeBroff as the leader of the Office of Public Interest Advising, she continued the fight for parity between corporate interest and public interest career advising. With the help of student lobbying efforts and a near-unanimous faculty vote, Shabecoff was able to secure a second full-time public interest advisor. She also fought to have the leader of OPIA be given the "Assistant Dean" title that the leader of OCS had. Today, she, her staff, and the students and faculty members who have backed public interest advising over the past decades have successfully secured independent office space, as well as even more full-time advisors and support staff.

Early on in their fight, one of DeBroff and Shabecoff's colleagues hung a sign up with the *Field of Dreams* mantra "If You Build It, They Will Come." It was prescient: When DeBroff and Shabecoff built out Harvard Law's public advising oper-

---

211 *Id.*

ation, more students responded by pursuing public interest careers. When ECPIP was formed in 1989, only six percent of Harvard Law students were pursuing public interest work after graduation.[212] By the mid-90s, that number had doubled.[213] Today, almost thirty years later, it has tripled.

The success of OPIA's development has demonstrated the connection between increased funding for public interest advising and increased public interest employment. And yet, OPIA's funding still does not match its task of: first, fighting against the grain of a culture and curriculum that pushes students toward corporate interest careerism; and second, managing the complex task of placing students at diverse public interest employers that, unlike their corporate interest counterparts, do not have the resources to share in the cost of recruitment. In seeking parity between public and corporate interest career advising, Harvard Law has come a long way in the past three decades. However, until a majority of our graduates devote their careers, as our mission statement impels, to advancing justice and societal well-being, the task is not yet complete.

The moral argument quieted

Pushback against the corporate interest path is also hamstrung because the strongest case against corporate interested legal work—the moral implications of working for a firm—is rarely surfaced in the career system.

To the Office of Career Services's credit, students *are* provided resources on assessing firms' pro bono commitment. They remind students of the reality that "the level of pro bono commitment varies from firm to firm" and encourage students to

---

212 Tara A. Nayak, Public Interest Squabble, *The Harvard Crimson*, September 30, 1989, http://www.thecrimson.com/article/1989/9/30/public-interest-squabble-pvowing-to-escalate/.

213 Susan Dominus, A Private Battle for Public Service, *The American Lawyer.*

seek out information on how to suss out whether a firm actually supports young associates' pro bono work.[214]

However, "level of pro bono commitment" is usually the limit to which the moral and civic side of firm work is discussed at Harvard Law. Professor Vladeck explains well what fails to be discussed: "How lawyers choose whom they represent and the consequences that flow from that choice is rarely the subject of any serious discussion at law schools . . . Seldom do law schools undertake a probing examination of the role that lawyers play in society and the choices that lawyers have to make in terms of how they spend their working lives."[215]

Take, for example, the "Law Firm Assessment Grid" that the Office of Career Services gives to students to help them assess which firm to join. The grid has 47 different criteria students should judge firms on, including "notable perks," "library," "mentoring," and "revenue per lawyer." Of the 47 assessment criteria given, only one resembles anything close to the civic or moral direction of the firm: "commitment to pro bono/community service." No point of assessment gets close to discussing the *actual legal interests* that the firm is advancing.[216]

Or take OCS's "Evaluating Firms for Professional Success" document, which provides questions students are encouraged to ask to firm recruiters to determine if the firm is a good fit for them. There are questions about day-to-day practice, like "Are they challenged by their work assignments?" and "Do they feel there are any limits to developing their skills at the firm?" They have questions about leadership and structure, like "Ask how teams are structured and run" and "Do the partners interact

---

214 See, for example, the web page "Pro Bono Considerations and Choosing a Law Firm" at: https://hls.harvard.edu/dept/ocs/jd-students/offers/pro-bono-considerations-and-choosing-a-law-firm/

215 Vladeck. *Hard Choices: Thoughts for New Lawyers.*

216 Harvard Law School Office of Career Services, "Law Firm Assessment Grid." at internal OCS site from: http://hls.harvard.edu/dept/ocs/.

regularly with junior associates on their teams?" Unfortunately, when a student reads the "Community Activities" section, the career office principally phrases the whole endeavor of community engagement in terms of self-interest:

> Aside from the obvious greater good that comes from community activities and public service, being an active member of the bar association, community board, or school alumni organization is a great means to network. It could be through these organizations that you meet your next client (or boss). Bar associations and pro bono organizations offer great opportunities to improve practical legal skills as well.[217]

Sadly, as is often the case, pro bono service to the legal needs of the poor is described not just as a duty in itself, but as a means to network and build skills so as to better position oneself in the hierarchy of service to the legal interests of the wealthy and powerful. And again, unfortunately, nothing is mentioned about asking firm recruiters about the actual legal interests being advanced in day-to-day work. Should not the first question to a firm recruiter be: *"For which interests will I be working?"*

Worst of all, the career system at Harvard Law occasionally takes one step beyond purported moral neutrality into actually encouraging civically dubious behavior. During my first year at Harvard Law, the Office of Career Services's website on the Washington legal market contained a document and podcast transcript produced in partnership with the legal recruiting firm Garrison & Sisson. In the transcript, a Garrison & Sisson representative directly recommends, in explicit terms,

---

217 Harvard Law School Office of Career Services, "Evaluating Firms for Professional Success." at internal OCS site from: http://hls.harvard.edu/dept/ocs/.

that students participate in the revolving door between corporate interest advocacy and government regulation. Under a header with a literal pictogram of the revolving door mechanism ("Government ⟷ Law Firm"), the OCS-endorsed document recommends that students: (1) work first for a corporate interest law firm, then (2) work for a government agency or department "that governs the activities of private sector clients facing specific regulatory issues" (which, the document reminds us, "provides contexts and skills to re-apply to the private sector"), and then (3) return to a corporate interest law firm to receive a larger paycheck as a senior associate.[218]

In the interview elaborating on the takeaways, the Garrison & Sisson representative explains further how Harvard Law graduates should first "learn how the law firm game is played" in a corporate interest firm work and then "get some government experience" for two to three years. During these two or three years of government work, he recommends that students work for the the federal agencies that "govern the activities [where] private sector clients are facing specific regulatory issues." To make himself even more clear, he recommends that students work for agencies that govern "the types of clients that have government problems *and deep pockets*" so as to develop "context and skills to re-apply to the private sector." Afterwards, the OCS-endorsed document recommends that students should "return to the law firm" with "government experience" in tow, allowing them to ascend to senior associate and receive a higher paycheck (one that is likely more than four times the median American salary) funded by the deep pocketed interests for which they conducted immersive research over the prior two to three years.

---

218 Harvard Law School Office of Career Services, "Ask the Experts: DC"; Binstock, Schwartz, & Donahue of Garrison & Sisson, "Washington, DC Legal Market: Spring 2015."

The OCS-endorsed recommendation reads like a corrupted version of President Kennedy's inaugural address. Instead of calling young people to work in the federal government by challenging them to "ask what you can do for your country," the Office of Career Services at the law school of Kennedy's university is directing students to statements calling students to work in the federal government for two to three years by challenging them to ask what they can do to gain knowledge and skills for deep-pocketed future clients. "The federal government," one section reads, "is a great place to gain practical experience and training." Indeed, the school frames government work no longer as service to our national community, but rather as experience to be strategically monetized.

Excerpts from Garrison & Sisson advice

14. GOVERNMENT ←→ LAW FIRM

Takeaway: If you wish to work in government and maximize the likelihood of moving to a law firm at some point in your career, the following reflects a typical pathway:

Years 1-3:   Law firm experience

Benefit: You receive training and substantive expertise. You also gain exposure to and experience with supporting the diverse needs of a range of private sector clients.

Years 3-6:   Government experience with an agency or department that governs the activities of private sector clients facing specific regulatory issues.

Benefit: You develop an understanding of the agency or department's perspective on legal issues, which provides context and skills to re-apply to the private sector.

Years 6-8:   Return to law firm as senior associate or counsel

Benefit: In addition to your government experience, law firm employers will value your prior firm experience with billing time, working with private sector clients, etc. In other words, you already "know how law firms work" and this provides a smoother transition back.

12. GOVERNMENT OPTIONS

Takeaway: The federal government is a great place to gain practical experience and training, and government practice generally affords a more predictable schedule than a law firm practice. For purposes of leaving the government to enter a DC law firm, firms are more likely to hire government attorneys with experience from the following agencies: (1) Department of Justice (DOJ) (i.e. the Antitrust Division or Criminal Division); (2) Securities and Exchange Commission (SEC) (i.e. Division of Corporation Finance, Division of Investment Management, Division of Enforcement, or Division of Trading and Markets); (3) Federal Trade Commission (FTC) (especially the antitrust/competition arm); (4) Food and Drug Administration (FDA); (5) Federal Energy Regulatory Commission (FERC); (6) International Trade Commission (ITC); (7) Federal Communications Commission (FCC); (8) Patent and Trademark Office (PTO); and (9) Department of Treasury.

Garrison & Sisson even point directly at the agencies with the most lucrative revolving doors, citing, for example, the Department of Justice's Antitrust Division, the Securities and Exchange Commission, and the Food and Drug Administration as "good platforms" for future corporate interest advocacy. They explicitly recommend against working for the Department of Justice's Civil Rights Division—which is designed to "uphold the civil and constitutional rights of all Americans, particularly some of the most vulnerable members of our society"—presumably because they do not primarily govern "the types of clients that have government problems and deep pockets." However, the document does namecheck the Consumer Finance Protection Bureau—the agency that Harvard Law professor and Senator Elizabeth Warren designed to ensure that the 2007 global financial crisis, which plunged millions into poverty, is not repeated—by saying: "We're already seeing demand for attorneys from this agency already increasing to go into law firm positions." Indeed, the law school which launched the public-minded career of the citizen who founded the CFPB is providing students with a statement encouraging them to work for it with the primary purpose of developing skills to evade, resist—or even, possibly, subvert—its mission.

Some may not find a serious problem in strategically planning one's career around monetizing their government work. But the organizations tasked with ensuring government and regulatory integrity take revolving door corruption very seriously. Almost every agency mentioned by the Office of Career Services documents as ripe for corporate interest experience is at risk of being captured by the very industries they are charged with regulating.

Two years ago, the Project on Government Oversight published a report, *Dangerous Liaisons: Revolving Door at SEC Creates Risk of Regulatory Capture*, describing how alumni of the SEC help firms avoid regulations.[219] In 2015, former Delaware senator Ted Kaufman, who chaired the Congressional Oversight Panel, said there was a "gigantic built-in conflict of interest revolving in and out of" the Justice Department. When lawyers shuffle back and forth between prosecuting and defending white-collar criminals, he told *VICE News*, it makes observers wonder "whether the laws are the same for everyone."[220]

The attrition rate from CFPB to corporate interest law firms[221] has raised concerns with the House Oversight and Financial Services Committee, which penned a letter in 2013 saying that "the close relationship between the CFPB and its former officials ultimately could harm consumers."[222]

In recommending that students explicitly work for these agencies with the intent of quickly leaving them to serve the interests that are regulated by them, OCS exacerbates the above problems.

True, the Office of Career Services is supposed to provide a frank picture of the reality of the legal job market. But at some point, a school aiming to "educate leaders who contribute to the advancement of justice and the well-being of society" has to decide if that frankness should come at the moral cost of, say,

---

219 Michael Smallberg, *Dangerous Liaisons: Revolving Door at SEC Creates Risk of Regulatory Capture, Project on Government Oversight*, Feb. 11, 2013, http://www.pogo.org/our-work/reports/2013/dangerous-liaisons-revolving-door-at-sec.html.

220 Avi Asher-Schapiro, How Eric Holder's Corporate Law Firm Is Turning into a 'Shadow Justice Department,' *Vice News*, August 25, 2015, https://news.vice.com/article/how-eric-holders-corporate-law-firm-is-turning-into-shadow-justice-department.

221 Megan R. Wilson, Revolving Door in Full Swing at New Consumer Bureau, *The Hill*, June 14, 2013, http://thehill.com/business-a-lobbying/305691-revolving-door-in-full-swing-at-new-consumer-bureau.

222 Letter to Richard Cordray, Director of the Consumer Financial Protection Bureau, House Oversight Committee Letter, July 31, 2013, http://oversight.house.gov/wp-content/uploads/2013/08/2013-07-31-OGR-FS-to-Cordray-CFPB-Rulemaking-Transparency-due-8-14.pdf.

implicitly endorsing corrupt practices. When a silent rule exists that ensures criticisms of firm life must be limited to its practical aspects (the long hours, the boring work) and excluding of its moral aspects (the actual legal interests that firms are advancing), a school can lose track of where to draw the line.

4d. A cost structure that dissuades students from public interest work

The elephant in the room—the most conspicuous reason that four out of every five Harvard Law students go on to work in corporate interest law—is, of course, the money. Over the past four decades, the ratio of corporate interest salaries to public interest salaries has more than doubled, from 1.5 to 1 in the early 1970s to 3.6 to 1 in 2004.[223] Indeed, any initiative aimed at having a majority of Harvard Law graduates pursue public interest careers must grapple with and counterbalance the stark reality that when a graduate chooses public interest work, they are choosing a starting salary that is at least $100,000 less per year than her classmates pursuing corporate interest work.

This does not, however, mean that Harvard Law School is incapable of better nudging students toward public interest work via the cost structure of law school. In fact, to its credit, Harvard Law has done better than most law schools in ensuring that the cost of school itself does not serve as a barrier to public interest work. Harvard Law's Low Income Protection Plan (LIPP), the first tuition debt relief program of its kind among American law schools, was established to ensure, in its administrators' own words, "freedom of job choice within the legal profession." It does so by aggressively subsidizing the loan payments of graduates who pursue low-income legal work. Critics have raised legitimate concerns about LIPP's treatment

---

223 Scott L. Cummings, *The Paradox of Professionalism: Lawyers and the Possibility of Justice* 8 n.39 (Cambridge University Press 2011).

of alumni with children, as well as the program's higher participant contribution requirements relative to similar programs at Yale, Stanford and NYU. However, for the most part, LIPP fulfills its mission: thanks to the program, most Harvard Law graduates have little reason to cite repayment on law school loans as a reason for not pursuing public interest work after graduation.[224]

And yet many still do. One reason this misconception continues is the choice architecture of student debt and loan repayment. Currently, students take on significant upfront debt during their time in law school. If they pursue public interest work after graduation, they can opt into LIPP, repaying their loans through pro-actively filing applications each year to the Student Financial Services office. Meanwhile, those who pursue corporate interest work after graduation need not apply to any program nor file any paperwork with the university about their employment in order to have their debts paid—they can just pay it off with their firm salary.

Whether this is proper choice architecture or not, it nonetheless helps entrench corporate interest work as the default career option. The loss aversion and inertia that come with setting a default option are again present here: first, students view "opting out" of corporate interest work as a *loss* of the default loan repayment option (high starting salaries) that they have been endowed; and, second, the extra effort needed to opt into the special, public interest path dissuades students from doing so.

One could imagine an alternative choice architecture of loan forgiveness that switches the default option to public interest career-building: (1) upon admission, you commit to a public-interest career in exchange for attending tuition-free; (2) if you follow through, then you never hold any tuition debt; and (3) at any time, you can file to opt out of your commitment, at which point the

224 Harvard Law School Student Financial Services, "Low Income Protection Plan", http://hls.harvard.edu/dept/sfs/lipp/.

school will transfer tuition debt to you, pro-rated to the number of years you worked in civic-minded, low-income employment. To put the difference simply: under the present system, a student takes on debt and can later opt in to loan repayment support for pursuing a civic-minded career; under this alternative system, you choose to pursue a civic-minded career upfront in exchange for free tuition, but can later opt out and pursue a corporate interest career in exchange for taking back your tuition debt.

The final financing could be relatively the same, but the default career options would be switched and all the built-in biases toward defaults would benefit civic-minded career-building. Students would view opting out of their free tuition as a loss to be avoided and inertia would help keep students on the public interest career path.

Harvard Law has experimented with alternatives like this before. In early 2008, Dean Kagan's administration launched the Public Service Initiative Program (PSI). The program worked as follows: students agreed, upfront, to be employed in public interest work for five years after graduation; in exchange, their third-year tuition was waived, in the form of a grant totaling their entire annual tuition. The program was supplemental to, and more restrictive than, LIPP: government, nonprofit, and political campaigns were eligible PSI employment, but private public interest firms and academic jobs were not. PSI was heavy on default option switching: first, students signed a ceremonial commitment early in law school to pursue public interest work; second, PSI students were bound to participate in public interest activities throughout law school, such as clinics, student practice organizations, and public interest summer employment; third, when participants' third years began, they signed a legally binding promissory note to officially participate in the program; and, finally, graduates in the program who wanted to return to corporate interest work before their five years were complete had to repay their 3L tuition at an above-market interest rate. Indeed, for PSI participants, loss aversion, inertia, and deference to authority were conspiring to hold students on the public interest track, rather than, as was usually the case, keep them away from it.[225]

Time in Eligible Position	Amount to be Repaid
Less than 12 months	110% of PSI Grant
12-23 months	100% of PSI Grant
24-35 months	90% of PSI Grant
36-47 months	80% of PSI Grant
48-60 months	70% of PSI Grant

In 2009, after the global recession had shrunk Harvard Law's endowment by 27 percent, the administration suspended new participation in PSI. Administrators argue that the program, which ending up running for four pilot years, possessed two major flaws. First, it gave funding to people who may not have needed it; the most economically disadvantaged students, after all, would have already had tuition reductions via a separate need-based grant program. Second, the program did not create any entry-level jobs in the public interest. As one administrator argues, "if students couldn't find public interest jobs, neither the PSI nor LIPP would work for them."[226] Citing these gaps

225 Erin Archerd, Public Interest Initiative Will Waive 3L Tuition, *The Harvard Law Record*, March 21, 2008, http://hlrecord.org/2008/03/public-interest-initiative-will-waive-3l-tuition/. For table, see: "Harvard Law School Public Service Initiative slide deck, http://hls.harvard.edu/content/uploads/2015/01/psipresentationsept2013.pdf.

226 Email to author with administrator involved in LIPP.

in PSI, administrators shifted their focus in the 2010s toward strengthening LIPP and developing the Public Service Venture Fund, which funds entry-level jobs in the public interest.

The experiment's success at increasing public interest careers is ambiguous. The PSI launched in 2008 and LIPP participation—a rough proxy for public interest career levels—doubled between 2007 and 2009 (from 51 in 2007 participants to 103 in 2009). This seems to indicate that PSI may have contributed to a surge in public interest employment. However, after the PSI was discontinued, LIPP participation levels remained high, indicating that other factors—such as changes in career advising or external factors, like the public interest job market—may have accounted for the 2007-2009 surge. On the other hand, perhaps PSI served as a shock to the campus culture that reverberated beyond its existence. More research is needed into the relationship between programs like PSI and public interest employment levels.

The story of PSI provides two important lessons to those interested in encouraging public interest career-building at Harvard Law. First, there is a wider set of possible arrangements to the structure and timeline of tuition and loan forgiveness than today's "tuition debt now, loan forgiveness later" system. And second, certain arrangements may do better or worse at nudging more students into public interest employment. To ameliorate a cost structure that dissuades students from public interest work, it is worth getting creative and experimental again.

5.

STEPS FORWARD
IN OUR THIRD CENTURY

To do our part to address the legal crisis of our time, mass exclusion from legal power for the vast majority of Americans, Harvard Law can and must counter these root problems in our culture, curriculum, career system, and cost structure. The Bicentennial is our shot: a perfect time to commit to the challenge of starting a new chapter where a majority—51 percent—of Harvard Law graduates go on to serve in organizations designed to advance the legal interests of the vast public.

We have been able to make such progress before. In the 1960s, a decade of awakened social consciousness, there was a decline in private law practice among graduates. In 1969, students turned the tables on firms, picketing law firms and probing recruiters about the "philosophical bases" of their work.[227] The law firm Hogan and Hartson even put out a memo explaining that they would face a recruitment crisis if they did not "respond to the larger problems of contemporary society."[228] There is no reason why such a moral revival could not be kindled again at Harvard Law School.

Other schools have succeeded in centering civic morality in their school culture. CUNY Law's 67 percent public interest

---

227 Seligman, *The High Citadel.*

228 Kahlenberg, *Broken Contract.*

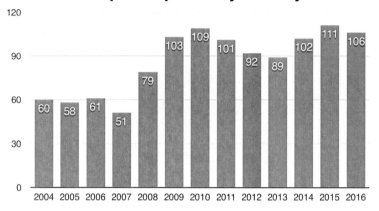

LIPP participants by class year

Year	Participants
2004	60
2005	58
2006	61
2007	51
2008	79
2009	103
2010	109
2011	101
2012	92
2013	89
2014	102
2015	111
2016	106

rate did not come out of nowhere: the school has made a commitment to the specific mission of "Law in the Service of Human Needs." As *The New York Times* reports, "Since its founding in 1983, the law school of the City University of New York has taken pride in its zeal to produce lawyers with a social conscience."[229] CUNY, one of the most racially diverse schools, is also the most welcoming to older students, and has a specific Pipeline to Justice Program to ensure that students whose LSAT scores are "incompatible with their promise" can be accepted without a decline in the curriculum's rigor. CUNY is committed to experiential learning, and its 3Ls are required to participate in clinics that serve the disempowered. Charles Ogletree put it bluntly:

> With all due respect to my legal institution and others, in my view CUNY Law School is the premier legal institution

229 Robert F. Worth, Dean Says, 'I Object,' to CUNY Law Students, *The New York Times*, April 26, 2013, http://www.nytimes.com/2003/04/26/nyregion/dean-says-i-object-to-cuny-law-students.html.

in the country and the world for training lawyers who are committed and dedicated to the public interest.[230]

Harvard Law can and should catch up to CUNY and become the premier legal institution for serving the legal needs of the many rather than the legal interests of the few.

With that mission in mind, below are 12 steps forward:

5a. Reforming our culture

First, we can reform our culture. Earlier, we described the problematic orientation given students at Harvard Law School—one of ambient competition that evolves into a game-oriented consciousness and results in a "cult of smart" enforced by rigid ranking. To change, we need a different orientation.

Reform #1: Measure public interest commitment

You are what you measure. As Dan Ariely explains in a 2010 *Harvard Business Review* op-ed:

> Human beings adjust behavior based on the metrics they're held against. Anything you measure will impel a person to optimize his score on that metric. What you measure is what you'll get. Period.[231]

When we, as a school, began caring about gender and racial parity in admissions, the first thing we did was: (1) surface the metrics of our gender and racial disparity by tracking the percentage of admittees that were of each gender and race; and (2)

---

230 "About", CUNY Law School Website, http://www.law.cuny.edu/about.html, quoting 1998 *New York City Law Review* article.

231 Dan Ariely, Column: You Are What You Measure, *Harvard Business Review* (2010), https://docs.google.com/document/d/1Rtg2p8msawzuXhMCROuv-GNwhDhTbNjdf7lCHPAHchI/edit.

set a goal of having our gender and racial diversity better resemble the nation's gender and racial diversity. This did the trick: today, after measuring racial and gender diversity in admissions, we have better optimized our admissions around that metric.

Similarly, if we care about a majority of our students pursuing work in the public interest, we should start measuring and publicizing how many of our graduates, over time, are pursuing work in the public interest.

As required by the American Bar Association, Harvard Law School provides clear data annually on how many recent graduates are set to be employed in each of the different legal sectors (government, public interest, business, education, law firm, etc.). However, there is very little consistent data on where alumni work years out from graduation. This is important information, because many students make employment decisions based on assumptions regarding the ease at which they can switch legal sectors. For example, many civic-minded students assume that it is common to pursue corporate interest legal work for a few years and then switch to public interest legal work later.

However, as shown earlier, if the ad hoc data collected over the years is correct, this common assumption is not true. Such revelations demonstrate the clarity and power of gathering data on alumni employment beyond graduation day. This is likely why Yale Law School consistently conducts a First Non-Clerkship, 5th year, and 10th year employment survey. Since Harvard Law does not do the same, our knowledge of the career trajectories on which we are launching Harvard-trained lawyers remains, to most students, shrouded in myth and informed by only ad hoc insight. And, more importantly, because goals that are prioritized are generally measured and publicized, the lack of measurement and publicity around raising public interest employment numbers signals that raising public interest employment numbers is not prioritized.

This could be alleviated by adopting Yale Law School's post-graduate employment surveys so as to consistently gather and publish data on each graduating class' first non-clerkship employment, employment five years after graduation, and employment ten years after graduation.

If survey data is kept in a way that tracks each individual graduate's career goals and trajectories, they may be even more useful in demonstrating how graduating classes move through different sectors at different points in their life and how career-building aspirations match up with career realities.

Such consistent data would make great strides in informing and clarifying student employment decisions following graduation, as well as administrative decisions in crafting admitted classes to ensure graduate career trajectories are balanced across different legal fields and needs. It is the policy foundation of a Bicentennial Challenge aimed at empowering a majority of Harvard Law graduates to pursue employment that serves the legal interests of the public at large.

Reform #2: Promote a culture of civic ambition

Harvard Law can do a much better job at centering messaging on the school's mission "to educate leaders who contribute to the advancement of justice and the well-being of society." One transfer student from The Notre Dame Law School, for example, informed a 2016 Student Government Focus Group that administrators and professors at his previous school had constantly emphasized their mission to incoming students, ensuring the students were persistently reminded of *why* they were in law school. He was surprised by how little his new school's mission had been emphasized since he transferred.[232]

The researchers Bonita London, Geraldine Downey, and

---

232 Focus group of transfer students conducted by 2016 Harvard Law Student Government President Nino Monea and the author

Vanessa Anderson have shown that law students internalize their school's culture within the first three weeks of law school.[233] It is in these early days that school elders can ensure that a message of civic ambition can inoculate against and transform the amoral, game-oriented impulses that tend to dominate student culture.

In *The High Citadel*, Seligman imagines such a message in an opening speech from a future Dean:

> You are about to enter a profession considered noble because under the United States Constitution and the traditions of the common law, it has an ideal of providing equal representation to all. No matter how great the disparities of wealth or talents elsewhere in society, both the adversary system and the democratic practice demand formal equality before the law. Accordingly, we expect you to spend some of your time working in a free clinic for disadvantaged people in this area. For the practice of law, we must never forget, is a monopoly. We deserve the security and dignity of our profession only if we satisfy the public's need of adequate legal representation.[234]

I would add that our Canon 8 duties—"to recognize deficiencies in the legal system and to initiate corrective measures therein"—should be emphasized early and often. In the same vein, I would add that the distinction between thinking like an attorney—advocating for specific clients—and thinking like a lawyer—taking care of the legal system—should be one of the first lessons taught to incoming students. Finally, a focus on our futures rather than our pasts should dominate early messaging:

---

233 Bonita London, Vanessa Anderson, & Geraldine Downey, Studying Institutional Engagement: Utilizing Social Psychology Research Methodologies to Study Law Student Engagement, 30 *Harvard Journal of Law & Gender* 390 (2007), http://www.law.harvard.edu/students/orgs/jlg/vol302/389-408_London.pdf.

234 Seligman, *The High Citadel*.

students do not "deserve" to be at Harvard Law based on what they have done; what matters is how students use the resources gathered here to serve the public interest mission of the school. Such cultural messaging can have a big impact on students and graduates. My father's alma mater was Antioch College, where the motto was: "Be afraid to die until you have won some victory for humanity." A few years ago, I ran into two elderly Antioch alumni. When I started saying the mission statement, they completed it for me and then talked about how they still live by it in their careers. *Imagine if we instilled the mission statement of Harvard Law School so well that when HLS alumni run into each other decades later, they discuss how best to advance justice and societal well-being!*

Reform #3: Spotlight civic intelligence
Earlier, I decried Harvard Law's "cult of smart," where those with the sharpest and narrowest analytical skills are held in acclaim regardless of their moral orientation. We should displace this cult by holding up lawyers who are examples of civic intelligence, rather than just narrow, analytical prowess.

The paintings and photographs of academic faculty and powerful jurists that adorn our campus walls should be supplemented by paintings, photographs, and quotes spotlighting activists and trailblazers. Portraits of Supreme Court Justices should be joined by portraits of, say, Reginald Heber Smith, the HLS alum who popularized legal aid for the poor with his groundbreaking 1919 book *Justice and the Poor*, or Jennifer Gordon, the HLS alum who founded the Workplace Project, a non-profit worker center which organizes immigrant workers and fights for stronger state labor protection laws. Campus buildings and rooms named after former deans, wealthy donors, and corporate law firms should be joined by buildings named after activists like Gary Bellow and Jeanne Charn, the HLS dynamic duo who set the standard for clinical instruction at American law schools, or Archibald Grimké, the HLS alum and tireless racial justice advocate who went on to co-found the NAACP .

Additionally, the experience and wisdom of living outsiders who made a difference in society as a lawyer should be integrated into the 1L experience. This can be done by supplying a steady stream of public heroes to interact with each class, not at voluntary lunch talks, but at mandatory section meetings. Students need to hear—together—from those who, in the words of Nader, "prevailed over overwhelming odds, primarily because they brought to a set of facts values backed by stamina, a sense of strategy and willingness to see it through."[235]

Harvard Law, for example, could develop a calendar of internal holidays to spotlight different heroes and movements within the history of the law. This could provide moments of collective reflection, providing the opportunity to teach the "why" of a legal career to supplement the more-common "how."

Finally, students, staff, and faculty who demonstrate moral courage and civic creativity should be spotlighted often. Take Harvard Legal Aid Bureau Faculty Director Esme Caramello as an example. When Massachusetts courts were awarded a grant to increase access to justice last year, Caramello stepped up to help lead the state's working group on increasing access to justice in housing law. It is often faculty members like Caramello—clinical professors and podium faculty who have extensive experience in the field—who offer students the best example of "advancing justice and the well-being of society." They should be the center of our school's culture.

The proposals above are all small changes alone. But together, they can help displace a hierarchy of prestige and narrow analytical intelligence with a culture that honors civic virtue and moral intelligence.

---

235 Nader, *The Ralph Nader Reader*, 381.

*Reform #4: Admissions should account for public
interest commitment*

If we aim to have a majority of students pursue public interest work and we are still not achieving that goal under today's admission criteria, we cannot simply throw up our hands and say, "there is nothing we can do." If we, for example, did not have a majority of graduates passing the bar, we would not give up: rather we would, in addition to other reforms, adjust our admissions policy. If we are serious about a Bicentennial Challenge to more than double our public interest commitment, the admissions office has to participate. It is time for us to more heavily consider "public interest commitment" in assessing applicants.

As Guinier explains, what the admissions office calls "merit" is a political question:

> Merit is value judgment and opinions about what virtues or skills are most essential to a lawyer or law student are as divided as opinions about any other political question. To say that a law student is meritorious because he or she does well at taking examinations offends those who consider a meritorious lawyer one who is dedicated to performing community service.

She continues:

> To argue that merit can be measured in terms of common legal skills such as writing ability, advocacy or organization is to denigrate such virtues as imagination, honesty, persistence, or compassion, which are not lesser virtues merely because they are more difficult to quantify.[236]

Of course, assessing any abstract quality in applications is an imprecise art. But if we have no problem assessing the

---

236 Sturm & Guinier, *The Law School Matrix.*

abstract quality of "analytical intelligence" in determining one's admittance to Harvard Law School, why cannot the equally abstract quality of "civic intelligence"—seriousness of devotion to public service and problem solving—be assessed as well? There is no reason the admissions office cannot better incorporate such factors in admissions criteria in the service of an institutional goal of increasing Harvard Law's public interest employment rates and, equally importantly, convening admitted classes that more vigorously enliven our school in the spirit of our mission.[237]

5b. Reforming our curriculum

Second, we can reform our curriculum. Earlier, I described how past curricular reform efforts, most of which resulted in increased second- and third-year electives, have been rendered moot by the 1L curriculum's resistance to change. To have a serious impact, we will need to build an integrated curriculum that avoids the "let them eat electives" escape valve.

In building that integrated curriculum, one has to grapple with an age-old debate among curricular reformers between those who say the curriculum can be more practical by supplementing the abstract case method with concrete practice opportunities, and those who say the curriculum can be more theoretical by supplementing the rootless case method with a historical and theoretical exploration of the meaning and purposes of the law.

These reform efforts are not mutually exclusive. Today, both efforts should be pursued—not as electives tacked on to a static framework, but rather as integrations into an enlivened first-year curriculum.

Two models are instructive here, both of which are derived from the world of health education.

---

237 Desmond-Harris, *"Public Interest Drift" Revisited.*

Reform #5: Learn from Gary Bellow's Clinical Institute model

In pursuing a more practical legal education, we have a lot to learn from Bellow, who was a trailblazer for Harvard Law's clinical programs. He liked to analogize clinical education to teaching hospitals. At teaching hospitals, he explained, there were clinical instructors, who would have their own cases, but also devote time to supervising and educating students in clinical cases. "Their instructor and practitioner roles mix," he observed. That is where his original idea for clinical work at Harvard Law began:

> We believe that every student would benefit from prac-
> tice-based instruction and that careful mentoring of
> course-focused student practice in teaching hospital type
> settings ... most effectively allows students to grow and
> learn. Our experience has again and again confirmed these
> premises.[238]

Bellow was successful at expanding clinical education at Harvard Law. But he dreamed bigger than a voluntary clinical program for some students. Rather, as mentioned before, he envisioned an integrated "Legal Services Institute," where courses would be taught on site at legal services offices and mix practice, social analysis, theory, and doctrine. He wanted clinical education at both the macro and micro levels.[239]

His original effort at such an Institute, he recalled, "really started down this path of an integrated experience in which you do housing work and study housing policy; you do welfare work and you study welfare policy." It was open to students from all law schools and required graduates to commit to a period of legal

---

238 Nancy Waring, "Clinical Education at HLS", *Harvard Law Bulletin* (1994), http://www.garybellow.org/garywords/hlbwin94.html.

239 Seligman, *The High Citadel.*

services employment. Unfortunately, it was shut down in 1982 due to cuts by the Reagan administration to the supplemental funding the federal government was providing to the Institute.[240]

In D.C., the Cahns proposed a similar model. Their Urban Law Institute began with a "boot camp" of intensive training in legal ethics, negotiation, and legal analysis in the neighborhood where students would be serving. Then year-round clinical work would begin, integrated with five months of normal first-year courses. School would be on a year-round basis and students would eventually rotate between three clinics.[241]

Growing a clinic beyond a one-off elective, Cahn shows, allows it to supplement "rights-based clinical education" with "powers-based clinical education." "Clinics of Rights," Cahn explains, are about vindicating specific rights in court. "Clinics of Powers," on the other hand, are about building clients' and client communities' power inside and outside of the justice system. When clinics are limited to being one class for a limited time, they often focus in on routine, individual cases that can help teach rights-based advocacy skills rather than systemic problems that can help teach powers-based tools of system change. To Cahn, both rights and powers are important, but it is the powers side that is too often ignored in clinical legal education. If clinical education was more integrated into the full three years of law school, the "Clinic of Powers" model would have more fertile soil in which to grow.[242]

Even incorporating the clinical mindset into standard classes would be a step forward. For example, the standard case method could be expanded to invite students to not only think

240 Hostetler & Bellow, Interview with Gary Bellow at National Equal Justice Library Oral History Collection.

241 Seligman, *The High Citadel*.

242 Edgar S. Cahn and Christine Gray, "Clinical Legal Education: Where Next? Clients as CoProducers of System Change," July 28, 2017, (yet-to-be-published paper).

like the judge in a case, but also to think like the lawyer who brought the case in the first place. Incorporating discussion of the litigation strategies of effective public interest figures and organizations into first-year courses would make great strides in centering public interest lawyering in legal education.

All such educational models above have what Nader once described as the two qualities required of a legal education: being *empirically rooted* and *normatively fired up*.[243]

Reform #6: Learn from The School of Public Justice model

In pursuing a more theoretical legal education, another analogy from the health education world is useful: the school of public health.

Until recently, there had been no conception of "public health." The discipline was previously a patchwork of efforts created to address ad hoc public health challenges with no unifying institution or theory. It was not until 1872 that the American Public Health Association was founded. The first school of public health was not founded until 1918, after an influenza pandemic with millions of fatalities.

The justice system is in the same state that the health system was in a century ago: a patchwork of local organizations to fight public justice challenges, with few centralized institutions or theories. Advocates over the past decades have called attention to a similar need for a concept of "public justice." Former deputy cabinet secretaries Thomas Ehrlich and Jane Lakes Frank have argued that we can minimize "common legal problems of the public through aggregation."[244] Susan Kellock of the Equal Justice Foundation has called for a "wholesale approach

243 Ralph Nader, 26 *Student Lawyer* (2007). https://books.google.com/books?id=hHE4AQAAIAAJ&q=%22Finding+a+public+cause+or+two%22+ralph+nader&dq=%22Finding+a+public+cause+or+two%22+ralph+nader&hl=en&sa=X&ved=oahUKEwiCxLL74zVAhXJzI MKHejRAdYQ6AEIJDAA.

244 Seligman, *The High Citadel*.

to access-oriented reform."[245] Nader, as mentioned above, has called for a raising of lawyers' visions beyond client advocacy and toward public problem-solving. Cahn put it best:

> Just as in health care, physicians are charged with increasing awareness of the "social determinants of health," we, as stewards of the legal system need to develop a heightened awareness of the "social determinants of justice."[246]

It is time to bring this concept into legal education and build a proverbial "School of Public Justice" within Harvard Law School. Just how schools of public health supplemented anatomy and genetics with the philosophy, sociology, politics, and economics of health, courses in a "School of Public Justice" framework would supplement, say, criminal law and civil procedure with broader questions about the law: *what is its history, what are its competing theories, where should it go as a whole, and how do the social sciences enlighten our understandings of its problems and paths forward?*

Guinier, Kennedy, Minow, and Rakoff's earlier critiques about the curriculum could be addressed in a School of Public Justice model. The adversary frame for conflict would be supplemented with "deliberative, legislative, transactional and collaborative" approaches. The problem of "sharpening the mind in order to narrow it" would be avoided by valuing the "social, political and economic context" of law as the centerpieces, not the marginalia, of a legal education. "Legal imagination" could be fostered.

Boston University School of Law professor Khiara Bridges explained in a *Harvard Law Record* interview how such a model could be realized through a first-year "toolbox course":

---

245 Susan Kellock, "A Wholesale Approach to Law Reform" - Chapter in: Robert L. Ellis, *Taking Ideals Seriously: The Case for a Lawyers' Public Interest Movement* (Equal Justice Foundation 1981).

246 Edgar S. Cahn & Christine Gray, "Clinical Legal Education: Where Next? Clients as CoProducers of System Change."

In that course I would offer various ways of thinking about the law ... I would offer theoretical frameworks for thinking critically ... about the law. I imagine in this toolbox course you will be introduced to Critical Race Theory. ... Legal Realism ... Feminist Legal Theory ... Queer Theory ... Law and Economics ... you would be introduced to all sorts of theoretical traditions so that you have tools ... so that you can go back to your contracts course and think about offer and acceptance in a way that is not like just like you are receiving the information ... I think it would be empowering for every student, not just the people who want to challenge ... I remember being in my first year and knowing that I didn't have the vocabulary to challenge anything that anybody said ... and I was silent. I wanted to think differently and I wanted to challenge the result ... but I just didn't have the tools to do it.[247]

Another way of realizing a School of Public Justice model has been the effort by Harvard Law professor Jon Hanson and Jacob Lipton to develop a "systemic justice" curriculum. As they explain, systemic justice courses focus on the problems in the law and their causes. They avoid being trapped by standard legal categories, instead turning to social science, centering context-building, and supplementing a litigation-mindset with other "incentive-altering policies and institutions." They train students to not just identify bad actors, but also build capacities in altering "the structures, systems, ideologies, and institutions that shape human behavior."[248]

And yet, despite their inspiring success at carving out space at Harvard Law for systemic thought, Hanson and Lipton's

247 Brady Bender & Pete Davis, "All Rise!", Episode 10: Khiara Bridges, *The Harvard Law Record*, July 10, 2017, http://hlrecord.org/2017/07/all-rise-episode-11-khiara-bridges/.

248 Notes from "Systemic Justice" presentation. Learn more at: https://systemicjustice.law.harvard.edu/

reforms still remain stuck in the "let them eat electives" reform trap. They serve to inspire students who opt into them, but have yet to make a dent on the 1L curriculum. If it is to have a significant impact, nascent efforts at building a "School of Public Justice" model must be integrated into the first-year experience, and not just for those students randomly placed into Hanson's first-year section, which is known for its public-interest focus.

A "School of Public Justice" mindset would not only serve to guide students—it would also inspire faculty to be more ambitious in their work advancing justice and societal well-being. There are a few professors at Harvard Law School who pursue large-scale civic projects: Carol Steiker's decades-long effort to abolish the death penalty, Lawrence Lessig's booster shot to the anti-corruption movement, and Charles Ogletree's ambitious founding of the Charles Hamilton Houston Institute for Race and Justice come to mind. However, the Harvard Law faculty has yet to bloom into the vigorous national sentinel of the justice system that it has the potential to be. Seeing itself in this more ambitious and dutiful role would be a first step in realizing its civic potential.

Reform #7: Incorporate practice and theory into the first year curriculum

A revised 1L curriculum could incorporate both above models. One could imagine a new first-year curriculum split into thirds.

The first third would be the current curriculum of classical courses in doctrine. In these courses, the standard case method would be supplemented with context that historicizes, presents present-day challenges, and explores future alternatives in the fields of tort, contract and criminal law.

The next would take lessons from the Clinical Institute model. It would bring 1Ls into contact with clients and pair their experiences with courses on the public policy realities that they are witnessing first-hand.

A final third would take lessons from the School of Public Justice model. It would merge philosophy, theory, economics, psychology, sociology, and problem-solving skills, training students to not just think like attorneys for future clients, but rather like lawyers, devoted to the justice system as a whole.

This, of course, would be a major change that would require experimentation and tinkering. One model to look toward as a first step would be Georgetown Law's "Curriculum B" model. At Georgetown, four sections are instructed under "Curriculum A," which resembles a traditional first-year curriculum. However, students can opt-in to one section instructed under Curriculum "B," which offers a justice-minded, innovative, and integrated approach to legal education. Instead of classic courses, first-year students taking "Curriculum B" participate in such innovative, contextualized courses as: Bargain, Exchange, and Liability; Democracy and Coercion; Government Processes; a Legal Justice seminar; Legal Process and Society; and Property in Time. Such a model, which has been successfully in effect since 1992, has allowed the school to experiment with justice-minded reforms without changing their curriculum wholesale.[249]

5c. Reforming our career system

Third, we can reform our career system. Earlier, I described how the career-building system sets corporate interest law as the default option in students' minds, nudging students away from public interest careers. To change, we need to end this default option-setting. To achieve this, there is both a practical and a transformational reform opportunity.

249 "First-Year Full-Time Curriculum" Georgetown Law, https://www.law.georgetown.edu/academics/academic-programs/jd-program/full-time-program/first-year.cfm.

Reform #8: Fund and promote career offices around the 51% truce

Students and administrators often decry the "public interest"/"corporate interest" divide. The public interest students feel that they are marginalized at the school. The corporate interest students feel that the public interest students are judging them. A Bicentennial Challenge—with a goal of 51 percent of Harvard Law graduates pursuing public interest work—could help bring a truce to the divide. We could build an understanding that some Harvard Law students would go into corporate interest law and should be aided by the school in their pursuit, while coupling that with an understanding that the institution, as a whole, aims for a majority of its students to pursue public interest work.

What reforms would come from such an understanding? First, there should be a concerted effort to avoid setting corporate interest law as a default option in the school culture. Professors should be encouraged to cite all legal professions, not just corporate interest professions, in their class hypotheticals. Career office names should be changed so as to avoid neutrality being associated with corporate careerism. First-year students who are defaulting to corporate interest law careers should be affirmatively encouraged to "try out" a public interest path.

Second, the Office of Public Interest Advising should be aspirationally funded. Rather than adjusting funding to meet current demand, it should adjust funding to meet the Bicentennial Challenge of a majority of students pursuing public interest careers. We should fund our career offices in line with our mission statement. The career office that explicitly aims to help students "advance justice and the well-being of society" should thus be funded more.

Finally, the dominance of the Early Interview Program should end. There are two ways this could be achieved. First, it could be eliminated altogether. There is no rule that a school must make it easier for its students to pursue corporate interest legal work: corporate interest firm recruiters can run their own recruitment fairs.

If the school chooses to continue facilitating this process, the date of EIP could be moved back from the summer before 2L year to the spring of 2L year to ensure that students have more time to think about their career trajectory before committing to corporate interest law.

At the very least, the marketing for EIP should avoid the appearance of institutional endorsement from the school: students should not be "highly encouraged" to attend EIP info sessions any more than they are to attend public interest career events; students not participating in EIP should not be pursued any more than students not participating in civic-minded summer jobs.

Reform #9: Supplement career-building with vocation-building

A more transformational reform would be to empower Harvard Law's career offices to take an affirmative role in re-orienting the student body's career-building efforts into vocation-building efforts. Instead of segmenting the academic, the professional, and the personal—as is the case today—the career office should attempt to re-integrate them, drawing professors, curricula, employers, alumni, and administrators into the process of helping students form vocations.

Angela Duckworth, the nation's foremost expert on grit, instructs us to trade *"What do I want to be when I grow up?"* for *"In what way do I wish the world were different?"* Those who have service-minded ambitions rather than lifestyle ambitions have career passions that last longer. They are more at ease near the end of their careers. They better avoid the psychodramas of competition and ego.[250]

At Harvard Law School, the career offices can take the lead

---

250 Angela Duckworth, Graduating and Looking for Your Passion? Just Be Patient, *The New York Times*, June 4, 2016, https://www.nytimes.com/2016/06/05/jobs/graduating-and-looking-for-your-passion-just-be-patient.html?_r=0.

in carving out space for students to explore these vocational ideas: of assessing what is important and what is not, of making commitments to things bigger than ourselves, and of foregoing options for the sake of doing what it takes to advance justice.

The career offices could establish routine, intimate, and mandatory events where students share their vocations or where alumni come in to discuss hard choices through a vocational lens. One simple way to take the lead is to encourage students to make a commitment to a vocation—like a cause, a community, or an institution—during their time in law school. Simply writing down what one believes can have powerful effects.

If such activities seem soft or goofy, we should ask ourselves why they are not too soft for the efficiency obsessives at Harvard Business School. Across the river, classes on leadership and purpose development are routine, and one of the most popular HBS programs involves sharing your life story and future dreams with your classmates.[251]

Under a vocation-building model, a public interest career would not be considered "a sacrifice" of a lucrative, "natural" career option. Moral arguments that supplement student self interest with other values would be welcomed into the conversation. Hear, for example, the argument of the Class of 2017's Simmi Kaur at a recent student-driven vocation-building event:

> A public interest job is not a sacrifice. You are not entitled to power that oppresses others. You are not entitled to wealth that further entrenches poverty and inequality. None of us are entitled to that and neither are our families, no matter how much we love them.[252]

---

251 See, for example: "Portrait Project," http://www.hbs.edu/PortraitProject/

252 Pete Davis, At the Harvard Law Forum: Letter to a Law Student Interested in Social Justice, *The Harvard Law Record*, Mar. 1, 2017, http://hlrecord.org/2017/03/at-the-harvard-law-forum-letter-to-a-law-student-interested-in-social-justice/.

Or take the direct messages of iconic civil rights lawyer Marian Wright Edelman regarding our public duties as citizens:

Service is the rent we pay for being. It is the very purpose of life, and not something you do in your spare time.[253]

Education is for improving the lives of others and for leaving your community and world better than you found it.[254]

Never work just for money or for power. They won't save your soul or help you sleep at night.[255]

Sentiments like Kaur's and Edelman's are rarely heard at Harvard Law today, but it does not have to be that way.

At the very least, we can better inform students on the data regarding happiness and the legal profession. As Lawrence S. Krieger and Kennon M. Sheldon show in their illuminating *George Washington Law Review* article, "What Makes Lawyers Happy?: A Data Driven Prescription to Redefine Professional Success," attorney well-being is much more correlated with what they call "internal factors," like meaningful work and autonomy, than with "external factors," like income and status. As a result, public interest attorneys, despite having much lower pay, were found to be much happier than corporate interest attorneys at large firms.[256] If we care about fully informing students about the legal profession, we cannot hide from these realities.

When asked by Humans of New York about the time he

---

253 Marian Wright Edelman, *The Measure of Our Success: Letter to My Children and Yours* 6 (HarperPerennial 1993).

254 *Id.*

255 *Id.*

256 Lawrence S. Krieger & Kennon M. Sheldon, What Makes Lawyers Happy? A Data-Driven Prescription to Redefine Professional Success, 83 *George Washington Law. Review* 554 (2015), http://ir.law.fsu.edu/articles/94

felt the most broken, Barack Obama explained that any time he was worried about himself—anytime he was asking "Am I succeeding? Am I in the right position? Am I being appreciated?"—he snapped out of it by reminding himself that "it's about the work": "If you can keep it about the work, you'll always have a path . . . there's always something to be done."[257]

Vocation-building is about discovering what "The Work" is for ourselves. It is about practicing the virtue of snapping out of self-focused questions so that we can return, over and over again, to the work that needs to be done. Here, we often ask ourselves and each other if we are succeeding, if we are in the right position, and if we are being appreciated. In the cutthroat era of Harvard Law documented in Turow's *One L*, we often answered "No." Today, in the pleasant era ushered in by Kagan's deanship, we often answer "Yes." But perhaps we are asking and answering the wrong questions. Our career offices should help us ask the right ones.

5d. Reforming our cost structure

Finally, we need to reform the cost structure of law school. Again, there are both near-term and transformational reforms.

Reform #10: Limit the real and psychological debt burden of students aiming to pursue public interest work

Efforts should be made to change the psychology of tuition debt and loan forgiveness. As mentioned earlier, despite the Low Income Protection Plan ensuring that few graduates need to pursue corporate interest legal work to repay law school loans, many students continue to believe in that false necessity. This misconception is likely due to the psychology of tuition debt: when tuition debt is taken on during law school, students

---

257 "Barack Obama", *Humans of New York*, http://www.humansofnewyork.com/post/110263143446/when-is-the-time-you-felt-most-broken-i-first.

are still psychologically inhibited by it, even if they have support to pay it off later. It helps set corporate interest work as the default option for loan repayment, because the high salaries of firm work are seen as the simple path to loan repayment while LIPP is seen as something one must "opt in" to.

It is time to re-open discussions around changing the structure and timeline of tuition debt and loan forgiveness. As mentioned above, the default option could be switched to public interest career-building if: (1) upon admission, you commit to a public-interest career in exchange for attending tuition-free; (2) if you follow through, then you never hold any tuition debt; and (3) at any time, you can file to opt out of your commitment, at which point the school will transfer tuition debt to you, pro-rated to the number of years you worked in public interest, lower-income employment. The final financing could be roughly the same, but the default professional options would be switched and all the built-in biases toward defaults would benefit civic-minded career-building. Students would view opting out of their free tuition as a loss to be avoided and inertia would keep students on the public interest career path.

The details would have to be experimented with, as they were during the Public Service Initiative experiment in 2008. Also, other factors might have to be put on the table to make such a system work, including raising tuition for students pursuing corporate interest legal careers and lobbying for tax policies that enable such a system to work. However, we cannot cite the complexities as a reason to ignore the standing challenge: to figure out a way to supplement LIPP, which limits *actual* student debt for students pursuing public interest, with systems that could limit the *psychological* debt aversion that students still have despite LIPP. At the very least, we should double down on efforts to explain to recently admitted students that LIPP will significantly limit tuition debt for graduates who pursue public interest work.

Again, lessons could be learned from the world of medical education. Peter B. Bach, director of the Center for Health Policy and Outcomes at Memorial Sloan-Kettering Cancer Center, and Robert Kocher, special assistant to President Obama on health and economic policy from 2009 to 2010, have proposed that, in an effort to increase primary care doctors, medical schools could be made free for $2.5 billion annually by offsetting general education costs with charges for specialty training.[258] A similar model, applied to legal education, could be to offset the cost of "primary care" legal education with charges for specialty corporate interest legal training.

Again, any change of this sort requires experimentation, insight from the financial services office, and a larger conversation. However we achieve it, though, it is time to set an institutional goal of having those 51 percent of students who we aim to have pursuing public interest legal work attend Harvard Law School tuition-free.

Reform #11: Lobby aggressively for civil legal aid funding

Beyond adjusting our own contribution to public interest employment economics, the law school could also take a more active role in lobbying state legislatures and Congress to better fund public interest employment. Anything that increases the number of public interest law jobs available to recent graduates and narrows the pay gap between public interest and corporate interest legal work will help to increase the number of Harvard Law graduates dedicated to advancing the legal interests of the public after graduation.

It was Harvard Law graduate Reginald Heber Smith who first proposed legal aid in his groundbreaking work *Justice and the Poor*. His proposal? Levy a tax on all legal profit to pay for

---

258 Peter B. Bach & Robert Kocher, Why Medical School Should Be Free, *The New York Times*, May 28, 2011, http://www.nytimes.com/2011/05/29/opinion/29bach.html.

legal aid. "Without equal access to the law," he wrote, "the system not only robs the poor of their only protection, but it places in the hands of their oppressors the most powerful and ruthless weapon ever invented."[259] Imagine if the Harvard community gave as rousing a call today as he did to the American Bar Association back in 1920:

> If we were to take command of the moral forces which are now stirring throughout the nation, we shall find public opinion ready to fight staunchly at our side. Let us assume that leadership by declaring here and now, that henceforth within the field of law, the mighty power of the organized American Bar stands pledged to champion the rights of the poor, the weak and defenseless.[260]

In an incisive 2014 *New Republic* essay, Noam Scheiber makes a modern-day case for nationalized legal care that Smith would be proud of. Most Americans, Schreiber explains, have improperly come to see legal help as a luxury good: something, like a Gucci bag, that you can have if you earn enough money. Even more, he argues that those who do fight for increased legal aid improperly argue that legal aid is like a social entitlement or positive right: something, like healthcare and education, that progressives find to be an essential material service.

But if legal aid is not a luxury good or an essential material service, what is it? Schreiber believes the proper analogy is *voting*: something that should be given to everyone equally in a democracy; something that is a zero-sum civic good, where

259 Reginald Heber Smith, *Justice and the Poor: A Study of the Present Denial of Justice to the Poor and of the Agencies Making More Equal Their Position Before the Law, with Particular Reference to Legal Aid Work in the United States* 9 (Carnegie Foundation for the Advancement of Teaching 1919).

260 Earl Johnson, *To Establish Justice for All: The Past and Future of Civil Legal Aid in the United States* 25 (Praeger 2014).

more given to one person means less given to another. He explains:

> If Bill Gates got three votes for every one I did, it wouldn't just empower him. It would disempower me. Of course, many will say that we tolerate disparities of this sort all the time. Gates doesn't personally get more votes than I do, but he can drown out anyone he cares to by spending his money on issue advertising or political contributions. At which point, it's worth noting that most liberals think this is outrageous. They want to stop it.
>
> In fact, because legal rights arguably trump political rights, equalizing access to lawyers is potentially far more important than campaign-finance restrictions. Political rights, like voting and donating to politicians, are about who we hire to make and enforce the rules we live by. Legal rights are the rules themselves. You could lose all political rights and still, in principle, live a decent, contented life as long as you had some basic legal rights (though I don't recommend it). If you lost your legal rights—if, say, you could be thrown in jail at any moment for no reason, or if fellow citizens could beat you and steal from you with impunity—it would be little comfort that you could vote in the upcoming midterms.[261]

There have also been less comprehensive pushes for increased national legal aid. There has been a long-standing "Civil *Gideon*" movement to extend the *Gideon v. Wainwright* guarantee to civil cases as well. The movement's main initiatives are, as summarized by Vladeck, to: (1) restore and expand funding to the Legal Services Corporation; (2) lift restrictions on the case LSC lawyers may bring, including class actions; (3) end the

---

261 Noam Scheiber, The Case for Socialized Law, *New Republic*, February 13, 2014.

lawyer monopoly on the provision of routine legal services; and (4) implement mandatory pro bono programs. Vladeck makes another comparison to the health system: *"Hospitals must accept indigent patients; why not law firms?"*[262]

There have also been efforts in Congress. Former Boston housing court legal aid volunteer and current Congressman Joe Kennedy III of Massachusetts, as well as Republican ex-prosecutor Congresswoman Susan Brooks of Indiana, have founded the Congressional Access to Civil Legal Services Caucus. The caucus arranges briefings to educate members and their staff on the importance of civil legal aid. Brooks has stated that the mission of the caucus is to make sure "that when civil disputes are brought to our judicial system, those involved, regardless of financial means, have access to appropriate legal resources and representation."[263]

It is time for Harvard Law—administrators, professors and students—to take a much more muscular stance toward civil legal aid funding. Harvard has not shied away from national issues before. In 1979, the Harvard Corporation denounced the South African apartheid system as "repugnant and inhumane."[264] Harvard President Drew Faust has expressed Harvard's support for the Development, Relief, and Education for Alien Minors (DREAM) Act and lobbied the Massachusetts congressional delegation to defend the Deferred Action for Childhood Arrivals (DACA) program.[265] We must speak out again—not just through the occasional op-ed, but through

---

262 Vladeck, "Hard Choices: Thoughts for New Lawyers."

263 Lydia Wheeler, Lawmakers Launch Legal Aid Caucus, *The Hill*, December 1, 2015, http://thehill.com/regulation/court-battles/261695-lawmakers-launch-legal-aid-caucus.

264 Jaquelyn M. Scharnick, Out of Africa, *The Harvard Crimson*, June 4, 2003, http://www.thecrimson.com/article/2003/6/4/out-of-africa-on-a-cool/.

265 Claire E. Parker, Faust Signs Letter Defending DACA, Undocumented Students, *The Harvard Crimson*, November 22, 2016, http://www.thecrimson.com/article/2016/11/22/Faust-signs-letter-defending-DACA/.

aggressive community-wide lobbying—in the fight for adequate funding to ensure equal justice is extended to all.

Reform #12: Lead a network of needs-based residency programs
In the medical education system, most students must complete a residency period before being licensed to practice medicine. Via a national matching program, students are placed in hospitals across the country to serve medical needs under the guidance of an attending physician. Residency programs are not viewed as vestigial add-ons to medical school. Rather, they are an integral part of medical education and the medical system as a whole. Also, they are consciously planned on a national level to support entry into practice fields and geographic areas where health needs are greatest.

In our Bicentennial year, we could take up the ambitious project of starting the process of mirroring the medical residency model in the legal education system. We could, together, set course toward a vision where law students, upon graduating from law school, are matched to legal residency programs around the country to serve, for a year or two, the most pressing legal needs of the American public.

Such a vision will only be achieved with coordination between federal funding sources, the legal community as a whole, and the entire legal education system. Harvard Law School—with its large endowment, wealthy alumni, and national clout—is best equipped to lead the way.

There are plenty of inspiring precedents to draw from as we design the first steps in the direction of this vision.

The first is Harvard Law's own Public Service Venture Fund, which awards over a million dollars in grants each year to help Harvard Law graduates pursue public service work right out of law school. Expanding the fund to a size that could support a majority of students pursuing public service work after graduation would be an a worthwhile aspiration in our third century.

Another precedent is the Reginald Heber Smith Community Lawyer Fellowship, which was hosted by the University of Pennsylvania Law School and lasted from 1967 through 1985. The program was inspired by OEO director of legal services Earl Johnson's goal of increasing the number of ambitious law graduates participating in OEO-funded legal services.[266]

The first class of "Reggies," as fellowship recipients would come to be called, consisted of fifty recently-graduated attorneys. They received five weeks of intensive, specialized summer training in law reform issues and were sent around the country for one- or two-year tours of duty at 39 Legal Services agencies. They returned to Philadelphia often to compare notes and build camaraderie. By 1969, the program had grown to 250 attorneys.[267] 85 percent of Reggies stayed on doing legal services work after their fellowship term was complete.[268]

Due to federal budget cuts, the program shut down in 1985. But we still have a lot to learn from the Reggies' experience. Mark Reinhardt, a Reggie from 1971 to 1973, talks about how learning first-hand what it felt like to be "on the side of the good guys" made him want to do public interest legal work for the rest of his life. Michael Allen, a 1980s Reggie, said the program taught him and his fellow Reggies "to look holistically at a poor person's needs rather than responding just to the crisis that brought them to our office." Leah Hill, a Reggie placed at Harlem Legal Services, explains what that "holistic" view means:

266 Alan W. Houseman & Linda E. Perle, "Securing Equal Justice for All: A Brief History of Civil Legal Assistance."

267 Robert H. Haveman, *A Decade of Federal Antipoverty Programs: Achievements, Failures, and Lessons* 302 (Institute for Research on Poverty 1977).

268 Earl Johnson, Jr., *Justice and Reform: The Formative Years of the OEO Legal Services Program* 302 (Russell Sage Foundation 1974).

Because I was a Reggie, my idea for legal representation was much more holistic, because problems don't come so neatly packaged as just landlord/tenant. Sometimes people have other kinds of legal problems they're facing . . . So being aware of that and also trying to find resources. . ., I began to develop a sense of holistic representation while I was a Reggie. It was my very first job and already I was thinking in terms of the big picture.

Allen explains that the magic of the Reggies was its focus on moving beyond funding job placement and toward building a mission-driven network of mentorship and fellowship:

A new Reggie-like program [should be one] that builds camaraderie, that connects people with a sense of mission instead of 'oh I got money to do a job at some far-flung place' . . . If the idea is not simply to give some people jobs for a year, but to equip them with the skills to really be poverty or disability or civil rights lawyers . . . , they ought to be put in places where people care deeply about mentoring and are very affirmative about raising a new generation of public interest advocates, rather than simply making sure these one hundred people get represented in a family law hearing this month . . .[269]

If a national residency program were established, it would need to be paired with a network of local institutions ready to receive placements. On this front, an interesting precedent comes from Edgar and Jean Cahn's writings on the "neighborhood law firm" in their famous "The War on Poverty: A Civilian Perspective" article. Their idea was to establish law firms in underserved neighborhoods across the country. The firms would be tasked with the mission of

---

269 All interviews with Mark Reinhardt, Michael Allen and Leah Hill conducted by Douglas Grant for this work.

representing "persons and interests in the community with an eye toward making public officials, private service agencies, and local business interests more responsive to the needs and grievances of the neighborhoods." They would be connected to nearby universities and would, like any other law firm, have staffs of lawyers, research assistants, and investigators to support their mission.[270]

At their 35th reunion, the Harvard Law School Class of 1958 created The Appleseed Centers for Law and Justice in a similar spirit to the Cahns' neighborhood law firm. The 17 Appleseed centers—spread out from Hawaii to Mexico City, from Louisiana to D.C.—aim to work systematically, challenging, in the words of Appleseed's founding member Ralph Nader, "the practices, conditions and regulations that underlie our social problems." They work with "community groups to identify areas of concern and develop solutions" through "a variety of working tools beyond litigation."[271] Each local center functions independently, but all are linked together through a national organization that supports them through training and technical assistance.

Appleseed's impact is inspiring. Texas Appleseed's advocacy for the de-criminalization of truancy, for specialized training of school-based police officers, and against out-of-school suspensions for minor incidents has chipped away at the Texas school-to-prison pipeline.[272] Nebraska Appleseed led the way on restoring prenatal care coverage to low-income children in Nebraska, regardless of their mother's immigration status.[273] D.C. Appleseed spearheaded an effort to challenge BlueCross BlueShield's excessive cash reserve holdings. In 2014, D.C.

270 Edgar S. Cahn & Jean C. Cahn, *The War on Poverty: A Civilian Perspective*

271 Ralph Nader & Wesley J. Smith, *No Contest: Corporate Lawyers and the Perversion of Justice in America* 380 (Random House 1996).

272 Key Accomplishments, Texas Appleseed, https://www.texasappleseed.org/key-accomplishments.

273 Victories, Nebraska Appleseed, https://neappleseed.org/victories.

insurance regulators ordered the insurer to spend $56 million on community health needs in the District.[274]

If one graduating class of Harvard Law School was able to build an international institution that has spread to seventeen cities in only 25 years, it is not naïve to think that all Harvard Law alumni, in concert with university endowment funding, could build a comprehensive residency network for graduating law students. What a wonderful bicentennial moonshot such a vision could be!

---

274 Mike DeBonis, CareFirst Is Ordered to Spend $56M on Community Health Needs By D.C. Regulators, *Washington Post*, December 30, 2014, https://www.washingtonpost.com/local/dc-politics/carefirst-is-ordered-to-spend-56m-on-community-health-needs-by-dc-regulators/2014/12/30/59a0378e-905b-11e4-ba53-a477d66580ed_story.html.

6.

OUR BICENTENNIAL CHOICE

A bicentennial is a time for reflection on the past, but also a time to confront the present and plan the future. Our past is a heritage of educational and professional leadership, coupled with adaption to the needs of the day. Our present is a crisis of inclusion in legal power. Our future is a choice: to serve the public or risk irrelevance.

This choice is not new: Harvard's history can perhaps be told as the story of its many declines and revivals of civic spirit. The future President John Quincy Adams came to Harvard during one such civic decline. The Revolutionary fervor had waned, and the sons and daughters of the Founding generation were turning away from the republican spirit to focus more on their private affairs. It was in that context that he gave a rousing graduation oration in 1787, titled *"Upon the importance of necessity of public faith, to the well-being of a Community."*[275]

During this time of reflection, it is worth remembering the message, warning, and hope of one of America's most inspiring Harvard-trained lawyers. First, he worried that the patriotism of the Revolution was being abandoned:

---

275 John Quincy Adams, "Upon the Importance and Necessity of Public Faith, to the Well-being of a Community," Massachusetts Historical Society, July 18, 1787, https://www. masshist.org/publications/apde2/view?&id=ADMS-03-02-02-0002-0007-0018.

Will he not be constrained to acknowledge, that the divine enthusiasm, and the undaunted patriotism, which animated the bosoms of his countrymen, in their struggle for liberty, has abandoned many so soon as they had attained the darling object of their wishes?

He worried that we were taking for granted our liberty and rights:

But what is liberty, and what is life, when preserved by the loss of an indolent carelessness, a supine inattention to the solemn engagements of the public are but too conspicuous among us: numbers indeed, without even assuming the mask of dissimulation, openly avow their desire to evade the performance of those engagements, which they once esteemed supremely sacred … Does not the very idea of a right whether possessed by an individual or by a Society, imply that of a correspondent obligation?

He worried we were throwing away our precious inheritance for a "paltry profit":

The contracted bosom, which was never expanded, by the warm and generous feelings of benevolence and philanthropy, may slight all public engagements for the sake of a paltry profit, but to a mind not bereft of every virtuous sentiment, it must appear that if any obligations can be more peculiarly solemn than others, they must be those for the performance of which, the honour, not of one individual, but of millions has been pledged: and to a person whose views extend beyond the narrow compass of a day, every breach of public faith must appear equally repugnant to every principle of equity and of policy.

And finally, he called upon us to revive our civic spirit:

> I am persuaded there yet exists a spark of patriotism, which may still rekindle a vivid flame. On you, ye lovely daughters of Columbia, your country calls to revive the drooping public spirit.

Adams added credibility to his message by living up it. He was a diplomat, senator, president and, showing a devotion to national service not shown by any other ex-president since, was elected to Congress *again* when he lost re-election to the presidency. As a post-presidential congressman, he cemented his most important legacy as the prime Congressional enemy of the southern Slave Power. He famously represented enslaved persons, free of charge, in the *Amistad* case, and spent most of his latter years fighting the "gag rule" that prevented anti-slavery sentiments from being discussed in Congress. In the 1830s, he presented a petition from twenty-two enslaved persons on the House floor, causing pandemonium on Capitol Hill. He was accused of breaching decorum and having flagrant contempt for the dignity of his office. Nevertheless he forged on, determined to do his part to bring about "a day prophesied when slavery and war shall be banished from the face of the earth."[276] Adams' young self would have surely been proud of how much "public faith" he later demonstrated "to the well-being of a Community."

A hundred years later, another Harvard Law graduate, Charles Hamilton Houston—the NAACP Litigation Director, Howard University Law School dean, and mentor to Thurgood Marshall who would come to be known as "the man who killed Jim Crow"—would put Adams' message more sharply:

---

276 Paul C. Nagel, *John Quincy Adams: A Public Life, a Private Life* (Harvard University Press 1997).

A lawyer's either a social engineer ... or a parasite on society. ... A social engineer [is] a highly skilled, perceptive, sensitive lawyer who [understands] the Constitution of the United States and [knows] how to explore its uses in the solving of problems of local communities and in bettering conditions of the underprivileged citizens.[277]

Community spirit or paltry profit. Solving problems for the many or pursuing rents from the few. "Advancing justice and the well-being of society" or ignoring our mission. Serving the public or risking irrelevance. In our third century, this is our choice. We have it within us to do what is right. Let's get to work.

---

277 Genna Rae McNeil, Groundwork: Charles Hamilton Houston and the Struggle for Civil Rights 84 (University of Pennsylvania Press 1983).

INDEX

Black Law Students Association 2
Bleicher, Samuel 101
BlueCross BlueShield 151
Board of Student Advisors 80
Bok, Derek 21
Boston Globe 14
Brandeis, Louis 17-18, 24, 27
Bridges, Khiara 134-135
Brooks, Rep. Susan 147
Bush, George H.W. 29
business schools 73

C

Cahn, Edgar and Jean 12-13, 132,
    134, 150
California 5, 28
California Bar 28
California Rural Legal Assistance
    28
Cambridge, Massachusetts 36, 93,
    102
Canada 30-31
Canon 8 of the Model Code of
    Professional Ethics 24-29
Capitol Hill 155
Caramello, Esme 128
Cardozo Law School, Benjamin
    N. 6
Catholicism 63
Center for Health Policy and
    Outcomes 144
Center on the Legal Profession
    49, 55

*Chambers v. Baltimore & Ohio
    Railroad Company* 13
charitable giving 40-43
Charles Hamilton Houston Institute
    for Race and Justice 136
Charn, Jeanne 127
Chetty, Raj 61
choice architecture 99, 105, 117
City University of New York
    School of Law 58, 59, 121-123
Civil Gideon 146
civil procedure 96
civil rights law 91, 150
Clark, Robert C. 106
clerkships 73
Cleveland 10
Clinical Education at HLS 92,
    131-132
Clinics of Power 132
Clinics of Rights 132
collective bargaining 67
Congress 20, 24, 25, 26, 29, 30, 87
Congressional Access to Civil
    Legal Services Caucus 147
Congressional Oversight Panel 115
Consumer Finance Protection
    Bureau 114-115
corruption 33
Covington & Burling 39, 43, 44
Cravath 75
Critical Race Theory 135
Cult of Smart 74
Cunha, Mark 40
Curriculum B at Georgetown
    Law 137
cyberlaw 2

J

Jim Crow laws 155
Johnson, Earl 145, 149
Justice and the Poor 127, 149

K

Kagan, Dean Elena 118, 142
Karakatsanis, Alec 6
Kaufman, Ted 115
Kaur, Simmi 140
Kellock, Susan 133
Kennedy III, Rep. Joe 26, 147
Kennedy, John F. 113
Kentucky 7
Key Largo, Florida 22
Klegon, Douglas 54
Kocher, Robert 144
Krieger, Lawrence, S. 141

L

Langdell, Christopher Columbus 1
Law and Economics 21-22, 135
Legal Aid Society of New York
    10, 41
legal apprentice system 88
Legal Realism 87, 89, 91, 96, 135
Legal Services Corporation 9-10,
    13, 25-26, 29, 32

Lessig, Lawrence 136
Lewis, C.S. 80
Life Magazine 19
Lipton, Jacob 135
liquid modernity 105
lobbying 20, 100
London, Bonita 125
Louisiana 151
Low Income Protection Plan
    (LIPP) 116-120, 142-143
LSAT 76, 122

M

Marshall, Thurgood 155
Maryland 11
Maryland's Legal Aid Bureau 11
Massachusetts 93
Mayer, Jane 21-22
McKay, John 29
mediation 70
medical schools 72, 90, 144, 148
Memorial Sloan-Kettering
    Cancer Center 144
Mexico City 151
Millennial generation 105
Milwaukee Area Renter's Study
    46
Minnesota 5
Minow, Martha 14, 134
Missouri 5
Monea, Nino 125
Moody, William Henry 13

Project on Government Oversight
    114
promissory estoppel 96
Public Citizen 107
public defender 49, 64, 101
public interest drift 54
Public Interest Interview Program
    100, 104
Public Interest Job Search Guide
    108
Public Service Initiative 143
Public Service Initiative program
    118-120
Public Service Venture Fund 120, 148

Q

Queer Theory 135

R

Rakoff, Todd 134
rankings 75
Reagan, Ronald 28-29, 132
refugees 64
Regiland Heber Smith
    Community Lawyer
    Fellowship 149
regulatory agencies 67
Reinhardt, Mark 149
Rhode, Deborah L. 9, 11, 14, 27,
    38-39

Riesman, David 96
Rohr, Joe 11

S

Sacks, Albert 92
Saez, Emmanuel 61
Sander, Richard 62
Sandman, Jim 10
Scharnick, Jaquelyn M. 147
Scheiber, Noam 145
Schiltz, Judge Patrick 76
School of Public Justice 135-136
school-to-prison pipeline 151
Schopenhauer, Arthur 75
Securities and Exchange
    Commission 114-115
Seligman, Joel 1, 126, 131-132
senior associates 76
Shabecoff, Alexa 107-108
Sheldon, Kennon, M. 141
Shell Oil 22
slavery 155
Smith, Reginald Heber 127, 144,
    145
socialized law 146
sociology 46
Socratic method 1
Solomon, Donald 67
South African apartheid system
    147
Stanford Law School 9, 117
Stanford University 61
State Farm 22